# TABLE OF CONTENTS

# Preface

The traditional news media faces an unprecedented crisis. The existing service model has collapsed, and the existing audience has moved elsewhere. In spite of the severe crisis, media workers at traditional news media are not transforming themselves. In some cases, they don't know how to change either their media or themselves. In other cases, they are afraid of the change because it is fundamental.

There are a number of books on media innovation. Most of them are no more than theories or insights obtained from other books or ideas. What we need are not only insights but also the practices required to change news media in the real market. I made up my mind to share my insights and experience to create and develop innovative news media from the ground up. That is why I wrote this book.

I have written five books about news media innovation in Korea in the last ten years. I excerpted the most significant ideas and cases from those Korean books, and edited to publish this English version, *Ground Up Your News Media*. I believe that this book will be helpful to existing traditional news media workers: journalists, editors, publishers, advertisers, and so on. They can find opportunities to understand the essentials of the drastic change that occurred in news media.

In 2009 I founded the news media outlet Wikitree in Korea. Wikitree was designed as a social-network news service, although at that time, we had never even heard of the word 'social network.' It grew very fast after linking Twitter and Facebook to one of the most influential internet news services in Korea. As of now, its monthly pageview is over 220 million, according to Google Analytics.

This book is about my idea and the challenges, experiments, experience, and bold action that have led to the success of Wikitree in the last ten years. I wrote the actual stories and insights longing for success in news media innovation. Hopefully, this book will help media workers for traditional newspapers or broadcasting services to overcome the obstacles that have held them back for so long. This would be a great honor for me.

August 6, 2019

Huney Kong

CEO / Publisher

Social News Co., Ltd / Wikitree

# 1. Media is gone

Social networks have fundamentally changed the flow of the news. The drastic decline of the media industry, witnessed in the case of The New York Times, which nearly went bankrupt, stems from the changes in the behaviors of news consumers. Social networks are not a passing phenomenon. They are changing the way people live. The Internet has become a part of life now. As the Internet led web pages and social networks to spread, social networks are creating other advanced platforms. Advanced mobile devices such as smartphones with multi-media apps create enormous possibilities on social networks. Just as the Internet did not disappear like a passing phenomenon, social networks and mobile services will evolve, fundamentally changing our ways of living.

The substance of fast-evolving social networks is content. News is one of the core types of content. Social networks naturally influence the news. When social networks change the way people behave, people can change the news market—fundamentally. It is because social networks radically change how people access, produce, and consume content. Readers who used to only be consumers of the news in the traditional news market are becoming the producers of and participants in the news.

## Social media closes the media gap

The advent of social networks had already been noticed a long time ago with the Internet. The long-tail phenomenon has existed in the news market for a long time. However, it came to an end with the emergence of the Internet. Social networks quickly penetrated the oligopolistic traditional media market.

Social networks closed the huge gap that the traditional news media could not cover. Traditional media, such as newspapers and broadcasting companies, have limitations in their "coverage." Covered news faces another restriction due to the limited space in papers or broadcast time.

Among members of society, how many have access to newspapers? Do broadcasting companies have them covered to bring them news? For example, how many among listed companies do you think will have a chance to be covered by the traditional media when they need them? Alternatively, we can look at the people around us. Sporadically, people around us, who are not celebrities, are covered by the media. It shows how people have limited access to the news media.

Let's say you somehow captured the attention of the media, and a newspaper reporter came to you for an article. However, newspapers have limited space. Broadcasting companies have limited time. The 30-minute main news is a bundle of sampled news, selected from various aspects of our society. Therefore, from time to time, we are bombarded with wrong opinions because of the wrongly sampled news.

The so-called "Pareto principle," also known as the 80-20 rule, can be broadly applied to the reality of the media. Traditional media, such as newspapers and broadcasting companies, can cover less than 20 percent. At the same time, more than 80 percent of the members of society cannot even get access to traditional media.

# Twitter, Facebook, and YouTube deliver friends' news

With the advent of the Internet, things have drastically changed. Social members who were excluded from traditional media started to voice themselves. People realized that they could express their opinions on the Internet whenever, wherever. The new technology of the Internet delivered their voices on the vast World Wide Web. People gave feedback by leaving comments on the news articles, opened debates online, and produced news themselves on blogs.

The new behavior of people on social networks started to cover the vast 80 percent media gap that was not covered by traditional media. The social networks that closed the gap include Twitter, Facebook, and YouTube. Thanks to them, people started delivering their stories and information to each other. They need not depend on legacy media. Now the links shared by friends on social networks consume the news produced by the legacy media. Bypassing the conventional news, which was often judged by the size of a media company or reputation, people started to select news recommended by their friends. One step further, news has become more about their stories than traditional articles produced by the media.

The primary reason the media industry is going down is that the way people consume news has changed. It's not because the media company's size is small or the quality of news is unsatisfactory.

The news that people want now should not be distorted by the political preference of the media company. However small it is, the news should be offered and shared for free, whenever, wherever. At the same time, an individual wants to put his or her voice in the news. Social networks, based on participation and sharing, have become a new way of life. They quickly closed the holes that the traditional media left out.

## They talk directly to others

In May 2009, Clay Shirky, author of "*Here Comes Everybody*," gave a presentation at the Seoul Digital Forum, hosted by SBS. He demonstrated the changing phases of the news media in three sentences.

"Media provide news to readers.

Individuals talk back to the media.

Audiences can talk directly to others."

The first sentence is about traditional media. Newspapers produce news, print them on papers, and deliver them to readers. The second phase is about the changes made through the Internet. Readers leave comments on the websites of newspapers and broadcasting companies. The third phase, evolved from the second, is about social networks. People send their voices to others without the news media.

Here, we have to pay close attention. In the first and second phases, there is the word "media." However, in the third phase, the word "media" is gone. News consumers no longer go to the media. They directly send and receive news. It means they are not merely news consumers. They have become news producers and participants as well. It strongly signals that the traditional media have lost ground.

In the three sentences in Shirky's presentation, the words describing news consumers have also changed—from readers to individuals to audiences. It is a significant point, explicitly explaining how the status and the behavior of news consumers have changed.

# All the media walls are torn down

Among the traditional media, broadcasting companies have the highest entry barrier. However, the barrier is going down now. Having a smartphone is enough to deliver news with video clips to anyone, anywhere, online. Many platforms enable individual broadcasting services. Anyone can act as the media and share news.

# Rising "smart readers"

People are already taking on new behaviors. The news media climate is drastically changing. Social networks reflect these new behaviors created in the wake of the Internet. Shirky's book "Here Comes Everybody" may sound scary to the traditional media. In the old days, there were only a few media companies that occupied the news supply channels. Now, anybody can become their own form of media by producing and distributing news without going through traditional media. Now, "smart readers" armed with high-tech smart devices hold the key to the news market, not the small number of oligopolistic media companies.

We come up with so many stories about people around us besides the stories produced by the mass media. Individuals differ in their preferences and interests. New technologies and services will meet the needs of these people.

# Everyone acts as the media in the era of social networks

Now, traditional media has become just one of the forms of media we use every day. What is media? It refers to a tool or platform where people can share opinions, thoughts, experiences, and viewpoints. In the past, it was owned only by a few broadcasters and media companies. However, anyone can share now. We call this social media. While Web 2.0 refers to the paradigm of opening up, participation, and communication, social media is the substance.

On social networks, individuals are all media. With a computer and Internet access, anyone can produce and distribute news. All the tools necessary to create news are equipped in most PCs by default. The storage for news is almost limitless. The medium, which delivers the news to readers in real-time, is free. Social networks play this role. They let you know the feedback of readers in real-time. It is beyond the limitations of traditional media.

What kind of role should the news media take while social networks have emerged for the media gap? Media companies who are ready to answer the questions below will be able to survive in the era of social networks. Instead, they will find a new opportunity and open a new market.

- Is there space where the traditional media can participate in social networks?

- How should traditional media cover the world of social networks as news?

- Can traditional media follow how social networks openly and directly communicate with audiences?

A transition from traditional media to social news media will open big opportunities and more possibilities.

# Baekdal diagram

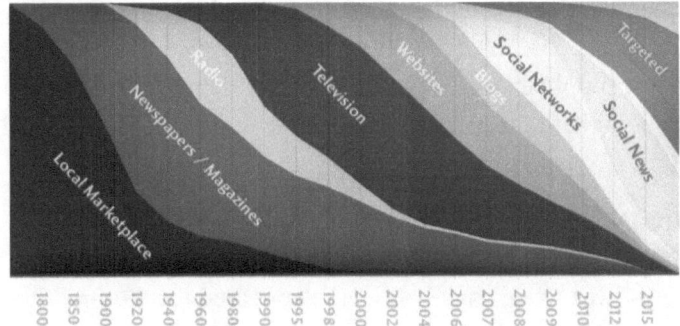

We can see the proper definition of social news and its prospects at Thomas Baekdal's entry, "Where is Everyone?" on his blog, *baekdal.com*, written on April 2009. Baekdal put all the changes of the news media into a single diagram. The title makes an interesting comparison to Shirky's book, *Here Comes Everybody*. While Shirky focused on the participation of people in the news, Baekdal concentrates on the behavior of people as news consumers.

Baekdal's diagram shows the changes in the news media. While blogs were popular from 2006 to 2009, social networks exponentially increased from 2007 and peaked in 2009. What we have to look closely at is the era of social news, coming to the next of social networks. Social news increased from 2010 and is dominating the news media in 2015.

# Newspapers and magazines shrinking

 In the old days, people used to exchange news at a market place when there was no newspaper or magazine. News spreads mouth to mouth in the market. In the 19th century, people gathered the words and printed them out on paper to distribute the news. The heyday of newspapers and magazines lasted a long time—almost 150 years—until they faced a drastic decline in the 2000s. The first medium that penetrated the newspaper and magazine sector was radio. However, with the advent of TV, radio could not maintain its market share. The golden era of TV was disturbed by the Internet; websites quickly ate out TV's turf. Since then, Internet-based new media have evolved.

Internet-based media companies, which have emerged since 2004 in earnest, completely changed the news environment. The era of excessive news supply has begun. Until then, the news media made the news and gave them to readers. Readers could not find news anywhere else. However, websites made the news supply exceed news demand for the first time. Readers no longer consider what to read. They now think about what not to read.

## From blogs to social news

The year 2004 was when social networks appeared for the first time, and they were mostly blogs. Without any specific technique, anyone could tell their stories on the Internet, which transformed from being a tool for experts to being a space for everyone.

The Internet rapidly evolved. After 2000, we witnessed the changes in the media in steep curves in a tight timeline. Blogs ignited people's desire to participate. Almost everyone created their own space and directly connected to their friends. People realized that the traditional media were very passive. They wanted to live the news—not just watch it but participate. It was how social networks opened up a new era. Then, newspapers faced uphill battles to survive.

The next phase is the era of social news. Baekdal defines social news as following; News is not reported by journalists anymore. The news comes from the people who make the news. Social news comes from the news source without any filter.

## "Targeted information," the last evolvement of social news

With the era of social news, TV viewing time will be drastically reduced. If TV broadcasting companies make programs and unilaterally send them to viewers, they will lose ground. Deciding what programs should be sent out on what time will be a waste of time. Viewers themselves will decide what to watch and when.

On the next stage, social news will evolve as "targeted information." "Targeted" means that selected information shows up based on my location on my mobile. With the speedy distribution of mobile devices, including smartphones, the era of targeted information has begun, and it's spreading fast. Here is a significant aspect of this. It is not "targeted news" but "targeted information." What is the difference? The difference lies in how traditional media defined news. It is meaningless for news consumers what should be named news, information, or ads. Everything is just information. They consume "information" but do not care whether it is news or advertisements, as long as the information is not false or exaggerated. Facts are naturally checked on social networks, and misleading information is filtered out.

Baekdal's diagram gives a good insight into the news media's changing phases. The year 2010 is when social networks passed the peak, and social news started to take over. Baekdal said, "everything is social" in 2009 and declared that "traditional media will die out by 2020." Newspapers printed on the paper will not exist anymore, and TV broadcasting will be broken into individual unit programs so that viewers can watch them whenever they want to. Radio broadcasting will be taken over by podcasts and vodcasts. Among the media, social news will be the most important communication tool. Thanks to the targeted information, numerous social news will be filtered out to consumers and bring about an efficient era.

News media is changing at such a high speed that no one ever experienced before. The traditional media are getting lost. They think readers have gone, but they have not. The precise point is that news consumers are still around. It is just that news consumers are changing fast, and the media tools that they use are changing. News consumers still exist. They still consume news; they just receive it in a new way. They are just leaving the traditional media and moving to another place. The traditional media are not moving fast enough.

# Advice from media gurus

Social networks have brought about a fundamental change in the news media. The new media paradigm, social media, directly influences the production of news and its distribution. We have already been notified of the change.

World-famous media gurus have repeatedly stressed the need for and irreversibility of new media.

## Perfect storm coming

Martin Sorrell, CEO of British advertising company WPP plc, said the media industry would have to face a "perfect storm." As the head of the multinational public relations firm, Sorrell has a knack for catching changes in the media.

The term, perfect storm, first appeared in Don Tapscott's book *Wikinomics*. He said that the coming together of a global platform for collaboration would drive significant changes in the media's content production.

## Citizens participate in journalism

Charlie Beckett, director of Polis, the journalism think-tank at the London School of Economics and Political Science, pointed out that news consumers should be given a chance to participate in journalism.

He criticized that the traditional media are still holding on to their old ways, trying to enlighten readers and lead opinions. It is because they see news as their product, made by the authority of the media, and regard readers as someone to teach. Beckett gives striking advice to the media that they should allow ordinary citizens to participate in the production and retail of the news.

## Context supplier makes money

In *Wikinomics*, Tapscott took one step further to say that the media needs collaboration with the readers to make money.

If readers take part in the production of news, they will develop loyalty to the news media. It is because readers find it natural to think that they can participate in making news content in the era of social networks. The news media can discover new profit models in this process.

# Create space for collective intelligence

Charles Leadbeater, the author of "*We Think*," offers a bigger and more detailed picture in his book. His point is that participation, recommended by Beckett or Tapscott, is not enough. Leadbeater suggests collaboration to make a detailed product. Participants can grow while copying others, helping them, and criticizing them. It refers to the typical relationship on social networks. Wiki-based behaviors are its most outstanding result. Mutual relationship and collaboration created Wikipedia and Unix, the cooperating computer system. In the area of "news reporting," Leadbeater recommends a whole new behavior through participation, mutual relationship, and collaboration. He said even an epic could appear this way.

# "Digital canvas" that anyone can paint over

Tapscott's book, '*Wikinomics*,' gave more details on how news can be created in collaboration. Tapscott suggested news can be a canvas anyone can paint over. He said we should not provide readers already-made news but an empty digital canvas. Upon it, there are no authoritative lines that the traditional media used to keep. The authoritative lines should be gone.

# SuperMedia completed by networked journalism

Beckett of Polis gives us a critical point in his book "*SuperMedia: Saving Journalism So It Can Save the World*." Existing media companies should heed their call. Beckett's issue is SuperMedia. His interest lies in investigative reporting. For an excellent investigative report, "networked journalism" is a must, he said. By networked journalism, he meant a collaborative system where citizens, professionals, and journalists all participate in the creation of news.

Besides human resources, networked journalism needs technical aspects. It includes new Internet-related things, including social networks. Beckett said new Web 2.0 technologies should be the essential part, not just add-ons, in networked journalism. Do websites run by traditional media put citizens' pages or blogs as an essential service? Is there any news website that openly looks for news sources or produces news in collaboration with citizens? Do they make use of social networks while they repeatedly report that social networks are changing the world on their news pages? How many of them use social networks as an essential part of their work?

The answer will be mostly "No." Almost all of them put those pages as complimentary service or do not use them at all. The traditional media have not changed. The behaviors and desires of news consumers have changed, but the media, which should have changed a long time ago, have not changed at all. Thus, traditional media are giving way to new competitors. Now newcomers, armed with creative service models, are entering the media industry to challenge the news sector and express themselves as the new news media.

# 2. What in the world is SNS?

## Media industry back to word-of-mouth era

They say the social network is a "revolution" or a major "game-changer" in the media. However, these expressions fall short of what social network means. Revolution refers to a sudden, extreme, or complete change in the way people live and work, according to Merriam-Webster dictionary.

Social networks not only changed the base of our society but relationships among social members. For this reason, the change is more fundamental and brings far-reaching repercussions than a revolution.

Social networks sent first shock waves to the traditional news media. The first news media in human history was "Word-of-Mouth." People used to gather around the market or on the streets to share news, and the news spread through word-of-mouth. Calling this "media" might sound strange. However, the word-of-mouth form of the media looks just like today's social media. Later in the middle of the 18th century, print media such as newspapers and magazines appeared. Since then, the news media's oligopoly has begun.

The oligopoly of the news media refers to several media companies' domination of news distribution channels through which one individual sends voices to the mass media. The oligopoly started to diversify with new media, including radio, TV, internet, and newspapers. TV, in particular, has maintained its dominant status in terms of propagation and addictiveness.

There was a decisive factor in why several mass media platforms were able to dominate the news market, and that is because they made the news quickly and widely reached audiences. The speed and the scope of news dissemination remarkably surpassed those of word of mouth.

The news media secured a medium that is much faster and more spreadable than the medium of individual-based word of mouth. The news media's medium included reporters, types, press machines, and distribution networks. Radio stations and TV broadcasting companies also had reporters, technicians, costly broadcasting equipment, and government-approved frequencies. Internet newspapers had reporters, websites, hosting server systems, large storage bandwidths, and links to internet portals that were distinctive from individuals.

## There is no overhead expense on social media

Social networks took away the "distinctive factors" owned by the traditional mass media. Anyone who has an email account can create a social network account without any cost. Having a social network account means having a medium to build one's power on social media. The medium that traditional media once exclusively had is now open to everyone. Types and press machines of newspapers have already lost their meaning. The internet has replaced distribution networks. Now, the speed and the propagation power of social media are much stronger than those of the traditional media.

Equipment to produce broadcasting content has become readily available thanks to the advancement of computers and smart devices. Broadcasting content distribution networks that host and stream extensive data, such as audio and video files, are not exclusively owned by broadcasting stations anymore. Video-hosting platforms such as YouTube and Vimeo are everywhere, for free.

Video editing software that used to be very pricey is now affordable or free of charge. Users do not even need frequencies that were a prerequisite for broadcasting in the past. Frequencies, the one-way system to send broadcasting content to consumers, do not meet the needs of consumers of social content because social content has to reflect other users' opinions. Broadcasting frequencies, once managed with state resources, now belong to data communication bands owned by private network operators.

Internet newspapers face a similar crisis. General and open-to-anyone web pages have replaced news websites developed and managed by internet newspapers in the social media era. Platforms like Twitter and Facebook have become a standard, offering a common user interface to all users. Internet newspapers operate expensive servers and pay fees for using communication bands. Building a website costs a lot, too. Moreover, to spread their own news stories widely, they depend on internet portals.

Social media users do not have an overhead expense. They do not need to build a homepage, operate a server, or get outside help from portals. They already have propagation power on social media. The information will spread depending on the value of the content, individual efforts to run the social media accounts, and sincerity. Power does not build up on big money and human resources. It never grows without genuinely understanding the culture of social media and carefully responding to social reactions. It takes time. While lots of resources, including a vast amount of capital and workforce, are needed to build traditional media, social media does not require them. Power on social media will be enhanced by sincerity, not by money.

## Highly networked society intertwined by smart devices

Smart devices have fueled the revolutionary change in society brought about by social media. Internet-connected computers or smart devices, such as smartphones and tablet PCs, have replaced news production tools. Smart devices created a new storytelling method, which the traditional media could not even imagine.

News-making factors handled by the traditional media were texts, pictures, and video and audio clips. However, smart devices enabled new formats, including taking photos, slide shows, interactive maps, polls, augmented reality, and QR codes. The "gyroscope sensing" of the iPhone combined with new content may result in a new style of storytelling or an authentic social ad.

Thanks to mobility and portability, smart devices also brought a considerable change by grouping every individual on networks. Now, "highly-networked society" has opened up where individuals carry smart devices to have direct conversations and send messages to unknown users.

Smart devices redirected the news production and distribution system from the old media to individual users' pockets. There are people in the scenes of incidents, and their hands carry smart devices. There are not many incidents that can get away with this highly-intertwined social network. When the US special army carried out a highly classified operation to kill Osama bin Laden, the founder of Islamist militant group al-Qaeda, people tweeted about "a strange happening" in Pakistan after witnessing a helicopter passing over in the middle of the night.

## The real legacy of Steve Jobs

There are so many legacies Steve Jobs had left. He deserves to be called "Leonardo da Vinci." He made a personal computer for the first time and gave them to friends as a gift, and applied the graphic to NeXT computers with object-oriented programming. He founded iPod and iTunes and created a networked world of digital music. He opened a new movie genre of 3-D animation with *"Toy Story."* Finally, he disclosed innovative products, such as the iPhone and iPad.

However, those devices are not the most significant legacy Steve Jobs had left. Smart devices like the iPhone and iPad dramatically invigorated social networks. People used to sit in front of a desktop PC to log on to social networks. Now they log on to Twitter and Facebook and watch YouTube videos anywhere, any time. They post what's happening around them, send pictures, and share videos with their friends on social networks. Steve Jobs created a new world of mobile social networks, and that is his real legacy. The new social, mobile environment has shaken the base of the traditional mass media industry.

## What in the world is a social network?

What is the social network? How is it changing the world? Social networks have changed the way we talk and remove the limitations of time and space when we talk.

Here is an easy explanation. What is the most frequently occurring and the most important behavior in human life? It is talking. We start talking as soon as we wake up in the morning. We talk with family at home, and with coworkers at work. If we need to make an important decision, we meet up and talk about it. Social networks enable these conversations in cyberspace, simply and easily.

Let's take the example of Twitter. Twitter has five major features. First, I talk to myself by writing on the tweeting window. Second, I respond by pushing the "reply" button. Third, I share others' tweets by retweeting (RT).

RTs generate the incredible propagation power of Twitter. Fourth, I talk to another Twitter user using "mention." There is no button called "mention," but I can add the other Twitter user's account name to the tweeting window. Finally, I whisper to another user, which is invisible to others, by using "Direct Message" (DM). Other features are supplementary.

If we take a close look at the five features of Twitter, we realize that it is our way of having conversations in real life. We talk, respond, share others' speech, and mention and whisper in real life. Twitter is an internet re-enactment of our daily conversations.

However, there are some significant differences between Twitter and real-life conversations. First, physical contact is unnecessary because it is on the internet. Second, two people do not have to find a time that is mutually convenient to have conversations. Whenever I want to talk, I talk. Whenever I'm available, I talk back. Third, I can have conversations with a stranger, as long as I follow the other user's account. Fourth, I can speak to many people at the same time. Once I push the tweet button, my posting is spread, not to a single person but many.

## If the media changes, the world changes

 Not only "production" of conversations but "consumption" is different on social networks. First, stories that I am interested in will come to me because my social friends who have similar interests shared it. Second, I can also spread stories to my friends if I find them interesting. In the old media, stories were just "consumed." In social media, however, stories are not only consumed but "distributed."

If the media changes, all of the world changes. If the communication method changes, lots of things change. The "open environment" where an individual's voice can be spread to many at any time has made traditional media's communication channel powerless. The change of the media will lead individuals to have different interests and ways of thinking. Then, corporate PR and marketing will find different ways, as well. Corporate PR, marketing, and political powers have depended on mass media. Corporate PR and marketing was the essential process to sell products or services to consumers. Politicians went through mass media to introduce their party platforms and policies to voters. Mass media is between people and these politicians or companies.

Without passing through mass media, the "one-to-many" communication is impossible. What happens if mass media is gone? What happens if companies and politicians find a direct way to communicate with people? Naturally, companies will change their PR and marketing strategies. Politicians will face a different shape of politics. It is not a prediction or a forecast, but a statement of what's happening right now. It is a revolution the social media era has made, a grand upheaval and beyond. Figuratively speaking, this is like a seismic P wave or primary wave has just hit. The S-waves or secondary waves that will shake the large and grand surface will soon arrive.

## To use the social network is easy

The statement is true. It merely starts with the creation of an account. When the internet appeared for the first time, people had to make homepages. Because it was not an easy task, homepage developers mushroomed. On social networks, we can create an account, and no more work is necessary. They have platforms that automatically find readers, make them come to us so that we can have conversations. Unlike homepages, which wait for readers to visit, social networks are efficient.

All we need to use to create a social network account is an email account. Anyone who has email accounts can create multiple accounts on social networks like Twitter, Facebook, and YouTube. Social networks do not require real names or usage fees. However, here is a trap. Because it is so easy to enter, people think the operation will be easy too. However, there is always a trade-off on the social network. Social networks require lots of operation know-hows after an easy entry.

Existing news media also made an approach to social networks easily. Of course, Twitter and Facebook are new channels for news distribution. They need to create a simple account, write news headlines, and shortened URL and send it. There is no sweat. Media companies even let intern reporters or part-timers do the job. Some companies send out those headlines at the time of newspaper publication in bulk. A little more sophisticated companies add "quotes" to the news headlines and shortened URLs.

What happens next? Tweets containing only headlines and shortened URLs are neither fun nor sensible. Fun and sensibility are two important characteristics when serving social network users. The media's editorial staff should change headlines to fit them on social networks and add quotes to make it fun and more shareable.

Let's say a patient social network user clicked on the shortened URL and saw the body of the news story, even though the tweet was boring. The news story has a rigid style and format that the traditional media have maintained. On the other hand, numerous content on Twitter and Facebook has creative styles and formats. Tones are all different. That is why social network users find the traditional news "too dry."

Let's say there are scores of news headlines put on social networks a day. To users, these are just "bulk," or even spam, because they might dominate the users' timeline at an unwanted time. Accounts that send out spam are usually unfollowed or even blocked by users. Whether it is a news article or a story, something on social networks results in reactions. The essence of social network operation is to monitor the social stream and adequately respond to specific responses.

On social networks, every reader expresses opinions on a news story and shares it with others without any barrier. In the past, readers' feedback was sent directly to the news creators – newspapers and broadcasting companies. However, in the social network environment, readers share feedback horizontally at the speed of light without a chance for media companies to intervene. If media companies miss out on the timing to deal with the feedback, their reputation might get severely damaged.

# Lessons learned from "Hotel Shilla's hanbok incident"

The corporate sector's current operation of social networks is inferior. Companies do not set up a social network account structure and operation target in advance but rush to make an account and operate it poorly. Their social networking is ineffective and counterproductive. They usually face difficulties in PR or receive lots of complaints.

Social networks offer an entirely different environment for the media. Companies must understand them well and get adjusted to them. Internet portals and social networks work differently. If you see social networks in the same way that you see internet portals, you will not understand them. You cannot just read a manual to understand the characteristics and working systems of social networks. You should take time, develop a sensibility, and accumulate know-hows to operate social networks properly.

If companies, media, and political circles want to make use of social networks as a PR or communication channel, they have to set up the precise structure, strategies, and targets. Individual users can have trials and errors to accumulate experience; official corporate channels cannot do so. One trial and error can damage a reputation.

The so-called "Hotel Shilla's hanbok incident" proved that one story on social networks could shake up a whole business group. The Shilla Seoul's restaurant banned a customer clad in Korean traditional costume hanbok from entering. The customer, who turned out to be a famous hanbok designer, posted this on Twitter. The tweeting instantly spread on social networks with lightning speed. The Twitter feed got more than 200 RTs and reached more than 1.5 million Twitter accounts. The Shilla Seoul, which faced fierce criticism in cyberspace, did not even have a Twitter account then. The hotel did not have any communication channels on social networks to deal with the incident. Numerous tweets criticizing the hotel followed. The hotel's only response was to borrow Twitter accounts from other subsidiaries of Samsung Group such as Samsung Electronics to post an apology.

The hotel's indirect response was not effective. The incident, which the hotel lost the critical timing to deal with, evolved to reach the National Assembly to decide to give lower evaluation scores to hotels without a Korean restaurant. The incident was covered by prominent overseas media as well. The incident clearly showed how an inadequate social media response would lead to a debacle in the end.

## Using social networks in the right way

The right use of social networks will reap fruitful results. K-pop boy band Big Bang's effective use of social networks helped the group rank No. 3 on a

Billboard World Albums Chart in just 10 days after the release of their new album *Tonight* on February 24, 2011.

Big Bang has not done any promotion in the US market since then. All they did was to post a music video teaser on YouTube and list the songs of the album on iTunes. Fans of the boy band around the world shared the teaser on other online sites, and people began downloading the songs from iTunes. The YouTube teaser went viral on Twitter and Facebook. The number of downloads on iTunes skyrocketed. The album *Tonight* ranked in the top 10 not only in the US but in Canada, New Zealand, and Finland on iTunes. Then, the album ranked No. 3 in World Albums on Billboard without an album cover.

Three months after Big Bang's album success, Korea's leading entertainment agency's concert in Paris hit the jackpot. First, European fans of K-pop idol groups of SM Entertainment uploaded a flash mob video to ask for a concert in Europe. In response to their repeated requests, SM Entertainment planned 'SM Town World Tour in Paris' where the agency's flagship acts all participated.

On June 8, 2011, SM's idol groups such as Super Junior, Shiny, f(x), and TVXQ arrived at Charles de Gaulle airport in Paris. More than 1,500 French fans of Korean bands gathered at the airport to see their stars. They were holding signs and placards written in the Korean language, and enthusiastically welcomed the celebrities and sang K-pop songs in Korean. The whole scene suddenly became festive.

Even though it was the first time that these idol groups visited France, they received an overwhelming welcome that usually goes to Hollywood stars. The fans were there not just for one idol group but a team of groups. Their craze at the airport showed the power of social media very well.

The airport scene went viral on social networks. French fans uploaded video clips of their first accounts with Korean idol singers on YouTube. International fans who could not be at the airport left comments on YouTube clips and other fans engaged in conversations there. One enthusiastic fan who had a concert ticket even said: "I will post concert scenes for sure." The fans knew each member's names of the Korean idol groups who have never promoted themselves in Europe before.

# Pop idols bypass TV

The TV was the crucial media for K-pop singers to ensure success in Europe's music market. It was impossible to let Europeans know without being on a TV entertainment show. Musicians had to be on every country's TV shows across Europe.

To be on a TV show, it takes tremendous effort and resources. Prominent agents need an extensive network of people and diverse lobbying, which takes lots of time and capital. If idols receive positive reviews on newspapers and other media after a TV show, they are expected to see a chance to be successful. However, to maintain their popularity, they need more efforts and investments because TV broadcasting companies stand in the way between idol groups and audiences. What if idol groups bypass TV media?

Big Bang and SM Entertainment did it. They bypassed the TV route. They have never been in a show on European TV stations. Their stage was not on a TV show but YouTube and Facebook. They uploaded their music videos and concert clips on YouTube. The wider the videos spread through social networks, the more fans appeared. SM Entertainment did "social marketing," operating its pages on YouTube and Facebook.

K-pop idols' videos bypassed TV stations to reach teenagers and youths in their 20s around the world directly. Not just a single idol group but the entire acts under SM Entertainment did this. If they wanted to see similar success through the traditional media, it would have cost an astronomical amount of capital and painful efforts.

# Girls' Generation in media

The power of social media does not stop here. Once set, "Customer relationship" on a social network does not disappear easily. Without a critical mistake, it does not shrink. Instead, in time, it grows. In other words, the number of Twitter followers or Facebook friends increases. The point is that we need to keep updating those social accounts with useful information or stories and keep talking with friends.

SM Entertainment operates a Facebook fan page under the name of "SMTOWN." Separately, it also runs each fan page of individual idol groups such as Super Junior, Girls' Generation, f(x), TVXQ and BoA. It is a good example of setting a Facebook account structure strategically.

The number of fan friends on social networks naturally increases. If there is a big event such as a concert in Paris or an announcement of a new album coming up, the number shoots up. The higher the number of friends, the wider the spread goes. It was natural that the international craze for K-pop idols went from Paris and London to Madrid, Melbourne, and Buenos Aires.

It would have been impossible to explain how fans around the globe copied the dance moves of their stars if we only had traditional media. K-pop idols have seen great success with little cost in global promotion by approaching social media differently. It is another strong example of how much power social networks can offer.

The "Hotel Shilla incident" showed how things could become uncontrollable after an inadequate response to social networks' criticism. In contrast, SM Entertainment's case showed how a strategic and structural operation of social networks could lead to great success. Here, we have a clear choice of which path to take. We cannot turn away from social networks, but we should not rush to open an account without careful planning, either. We have to come up with a meticulous plan on how to compose the social network account, how to gather or produce content, and how to organize an operating system. If you systemically operate social networks as SM Entertainment did, you will see low-cost, highly-effective productive results.

# 3. New Understandings

## News without a stream dies

Social networks demand a fundamental change in the newsroom's and reporters' role, as well as the sourcing methods. To maintain as a news media on social networks, the news produced in the newsroom should get feedback. It does not merely mean "Likes," but a stream that flows. If readers read the news and stop there, its value ends there.

In traditional media, the newsroom's role was to produce news. When newspapers provide news and print them out, they did not have to take care of them. Broadcasting companies aired their programs, and that was it. The lifecycle of the news ends once it is printed on paper or broadcast on air. The role of the newsroom ends after sending out the story. However, in the eyes of social networks, the news died as soon as it was born.

The news has to flow. There should be a "news stream." Traditional media should understand this concept. On Twitter, posts have to be retweeted (RT) over and over again. On Facebook, the news has to have endless clicks of the "Like" button and shared on others' news feeds. The life cycle of news begins in the newsroom. The longevity of the news depends on how wide it will spread since being posted on social networks. The longer it gets, the power of the news grows. The number of retweets and followers that retweeted determine the length of the lifecycle of news on Tweeter. On Facebook, the number of likes, the number of comments, and the number of sharing on the friends' news feeds do.

## It's not "stock" but "flow"

On social networks, we can evaluate not only the quantity of the shared news but the quality. On Twitter, the evaluation appears on added mentions as users retweet a particular news story. On Facebook, it appears on comments and replies. These mentions and comments are essential resources containing the subjective evaluations of the news.

News service on social networks should be managed to have maximum longevity. It directly influences the power of the news media. At the same time, the news media should collect data and reactions, while the news story is flowing. The number of retweets or likes shows how wide readers spread the news, and their responses are immediately visible. Managing the news on social networks is the duty of the newsroom.

Unfortunately, however, traditional media newsrooms focus only on news production. They have almost no interest in its distribution. While readers are consuming the news on social networks, there is no function within the newsroom to managing news streams. It seems like they have given up the influential power as a news media.

It is the same case with the advertisement market. Advertising on social networks does not end just there. That is the beginning of the advertisement. If the ad does not create a "stream," it does not affect. Whether it is news or advertisement, the concept should be "flow," not "stock."

## Social networks are not about comments

 Malicious comments are the evils of the internet. Cyberbullying, the act of harming an individual via the internet in a repeated manner, is considered the "murder of a personality." Malicious comments have existed in portal sites, community sites, internet news websites, and mini-blogs. Even if the site checks the real name, it cannot fundamentally block malicious comments. Due to the harmful effect of lewd comments, South Korea has a unique internet regulation that requires users' real names on websites that have more than 100,000 visitors a day.

Now, things have changed because of social networks. We rarely see malicious comments on social networks. Comments and social networks are different. To understand the difference, we have to look at the nature of the comments. Comments have the system of "one to many." For example, A is a massive portal site, and many users comment on the site. One of the users leaves a malicious comment on A. The user has this psychological mindset that "A, such a large portal, would not care about a small user like me." Indeed, it is not easy, or rather impossible, for A to deal with numerous individual users one on one. As long as the problem is small, A does not deal with the small user's evil comments.

On social networks, however, the environment is different because the service structure is different. The relationship between users is also different. Social networks are not portals but platforms. If we say portals are like a large bowl that contains users' stories, platforms are connected grounds where users give and take their stories.

So social networks connect many to many in real-time. Users instantly learn how many connections they have. Although social networks connect many users, you do not know who they are. Your acquaintances could be present among them.

# Cyber personality activates on social networks

 Many users connected to others and the anonymity of the many create a strong "police force" on social networks. We can call it "refining capacity" as well. Even though a particular institution or operator does not intervene, users themselves regulate each other's behaviors. These voluntary regulations have reliable control power, although they are not in the written forms. It is a new refining system that we have not experienced in cyberspace ever.

Social networks are platforms where cyber personalities communicate with each other. On Facebook, an individual has to open their personal information to a certain degree to get a wider network of friends. On Twitter as well, users open their locations, significant interests and, in many cases, real names. The more personal information is open, the more connections you get.

It does not mean that Twitter or Facebook check on your real name. All you need to open an account is your email address. If you have several email accounts, you can open several accounts on Twitter or Facebook. They do not care whether the name you use is an alias or real name, or whether you have one or several accounts.

There are more than 180 Twitter accounts registered as Steve Jobs, the late CEO of Apple. In reality, Steve Jobs did not use Twitter. However, several fake Steve Jobs put his photos on profile and upload mentions that sound like Steve Jobs. Some news media sent a wrong news report based on a fake Steve Jobs' Twitter mention. However, Twitter did not even care because it is up to users who judge whether Steve Jobs' account is real or fake. The order is regulated by the many — that is, "social." Thus, Twitter is, indeed, a social network platform.

## Truth in the hands of many

Social networks have a completely different principle. It is risky for an individual or an institution to judge news, whether it is true or not, and present it to many. If you make a mistake, it will not go away forever. The risk is high. Whether it is true or not, you have to expose your story to people, without adding or taking out, and let many to judge. It will produce more correct results. It is "social ecology." Those who are comfortable with the old authority will think social ecology is risky. However, the results coming out of the social ecology are precise, and the refining force will be strongly activated.

Twitter is a good match for "social ecology." Do we see Twitter users who slander other users, spread false statements, use abusive languages, or make vulgar jokes? Hardly. Even if it is possible to open an alias account or several different accounts on Twitter, malicious comments are almost invisible. It is because Twitter connects many to many in real-time. This structure has a reliable refining power. We have experienced it on the internet. On social networks, the concept of malicious comments disappears.

People have used the internet since the mid-1990s. Social networks are a new platform, created based on the technology of the internet. This platform bore new behaviors. As internet users are used to new practices on a new platform of social networks, the "rule of the game" changed. Social networks' refining power is innovation.

## Business opportunities created in "social ecology"

"Social ecology" created by social networks gives us new business opportunities. Social ecology screens, whether the content flowing on social networks, are true or false or exaggerated. If the content meets the needs of people or the trend, it instantly goes viral.

On the opposite side, if the content is false, people figure it out through collaborations. If the content were put online intentionally, the uploader would face revenge from social users. The result is severe damage to the reputation in social networks. If the case is severe, the uploader can lose its "personality" on social networks and become ostracized. On Twitter, "unfollow" and "block" happen quietly, without notifying the user. On Facebook as well, if you block or unfriend a friend, it does not send a notification to the other party. However, behaviors like this spread at an alarming speed among Twitter and Facebook users.

The reliable power of the refining process on social networks gives the proper spirit to the consumer market. In other words, unless the product or service is excellent, it will not be able to persuade social network users to purchase it. At the same time, if people prefer the product or service and the quality is proven, it will be a jackpot even if the product maker is a newcomer in the market.

## Content should "flow" on social networks

Traditional media used a one-way method of advertisement. Once newspapers or broadcasting companies publish an ad, it is the end of the story. To find out how consumers reacted to the advertisement, they would have to carry out another research to get data, such as the size of the audience reached. Advertisers had no way to rely on a report on how active the ad was. However, in most cases, the publisher of the ad created the report themselves. Therefore, old ad models stay in the concept of "stock." They do not flow. If the media takes the order of the advertiser and runs the ad, that's it.

On social networks, ad flows. Precisely speaking, it cannot be called an "ad." On social networks, whether it is an ad or news or information, they are all content. Whether the content is an ad, news, or information, it is social network users who judge it. In the old media, it was the supplier of the content who decided it was an ad, or news or information. This process excluded readers. However, on social networks, the authority of evaluating content does not belong to the creator. It is up to people to evaluate the content.

To reiterate this, people do not care whether the content is ad or news or information. They will only judge whether it is fun, valuable, and recommendable to their friends. If the content explicitly demands the purchase of the product, people will reject it.

However, if they agree that the product's content is good, someone will find out how to purchase it, and the content will go viral through recommendations. The significant factor here is the "content." On social networks, it's not an ad, but "content," and it flows. The ad is just one form of content. On social networks, the content has to "flow."

The content has three significant characteristics. First, as has already been stated, it flows. Second, it spreads. Third, the flow and the spread of the content can be measured, in real-time. In the old ad market, we rarely saw these characteristics. Instead, the ad cycle ended before these characteristics even started to occur. As the ad was published, the lifecycle of the ad ended.

On social networks, the lifecycle of the ad begins after it is published. Other users move the content to share it or recommend it to friends, and friends of friends recommend it to their friends, creating a multiplier effect. The number of recommendations is measurable, thanks to open API, serviced by social networks such as Twitter and Facebook. On such a social network, we can measure specific content on how wide and how fast it spreads in real-time.

We can evaluate the quality of the content as well. While users share the content or recommend it to friends, they usually make a short opinion about it. On Twitter, this refers to "mention" or "quote." These mentions or quotes show how users evaluate the content. If there are a lot of mentions or quotes stocked, they are good "consumer reactions." And this happens in real-time.

## "Social ad" on "social stream"

The producer of the content can monitor real-time reactions to the content on social networks. It is called "social stream." Now, let's switch "content" with "ad." It is a whole new form of ad. It is "social advertisement" flowing in the social stream. The media should sell the "social stream" to advertisers.

I remind you that the ad is one type of content. It does not require the extravagant graphics or eye-catching copies that used to be present in the old media. Content has to have a message, something that will appeal to consumers by heart. Thus, consumers will find it relevant, recommend it to friends and purchase the product at the end.

Social networks have created a "social ecology" where many are connected to many. The ecology has shaped a strong refining force. This force opens the possibility of solving the problem of internet ethics in cyberspace. At the same time, this force gives new internet-based business opportunities. Social ecology is an innovation by the collaboration of networked people.

## Something new to me is news to others

What kind of news do readers on social networks likely read? Individuals participate in producing news on social networks. Without being conscious of news production, they let others know what's happening around their lives. No matter how trivial it is, they want their friends to know something new that happened in their lives. The content of the news is not extraordinary. However, something new is news to others. New things around me, something that made me upset, something surprising or to be careful about and other trivial things are good topics to talk about with family, friends, and coworkers. Those conversations are all news. Before the first news media,newspapers appeared, people used to share conversations at a market or on the streets, and that was news. The most primitive form of news is conversations.

The news that the traditional media have covered is just a part of the news. Let's go over the limits of resources the legacy media have had. In the first place, it was impossible to cover all of the happenings in the world on limited papers or broadcasting time. The news was a tiny sample of what was going on in the world. So, the media has a tremendous power on what, how, when to report, and whether to publish, or not.

Things are entirely different in the era of social networks. There is no space or time limit in delivering news. You can provide anything that happened around you to other users at any time, in any form, as long as you have a PC or smartphone connected online.

# Daily stories become news

When I was at a seminar, I engaged in a conversation with a female reporter. She was complaining about her dogs. She had two: a Siberian Husky and a Yorkshire Terrier. One day, the bigger one played tricks and bit the small one, but the Yorkshire terrier's wound was severe. She repeatedly said how she felt bad about it. I told her, "That's news." The story is informative, in that it is dangerous to put a large dog next to a small one. If she had uploaded this story on Twitter or Facebook, she would have received reactions like this: "I feel bad about the injured dog," "I hope the dog gets well soon," "We should be careful in putting the dogs together," or "You'd better apologize, Siberian husky." On the contrary, there can be negative responses like "If you don't know how to take care of your dogs, you don't deserve them." Social media is such a double-edged sword nowadays. As news, the content has enough value. Social networks limitlessly contain this kind of news that is fund and valuable and directly deliver to readers.

The traditional news media should pay careful attention to little things that occur among people because they like it. They should offer live news vastly and variously. There are still sectors that the old media used to cover— politics and policies, for example. There are also news sources that the media can instantly get access to. The media still has to cover these areas. However, if they fail to catch the attention of people, its news will lose power. It is a severe social problem that important news and information cannot reach people. The existing news media should innovate themselves to keep the attention of readers.

## Readers consume fun and value

Wikitree, which is an open, participatory media, provides content that could have been considered unacceptable to the traditional media. The content varies. It can be a parody photo or cartoons with speech balloons. Some even ask readers "what they think" about the story. For example, a parody cartoon of Apple CEO Steve Jobs and Samsung Group Chairman Lee Kun-hee on Wikitree showed a drastic difference in the reactions between readers and the traditional media. The series of parodies became the talk of the town, but no other media reported it as news.

# Parodies are also news content

The series of parodies of Steve Jobs and Lee Kun-hee is not just funny jokes. They have a clear message. The first parody shows the difference in marketing methods between Apple and Samsung. The second parody exposes the differences in the corporate culture between Apple under Jobs and Samsung under Lee. Let's say we will write a traditional news story based on these parodies. First, how many users will read it? Second, how many messages can it show? How many will precisely understand the content and remember it? Putting together several photo cuts and adding several speech balloons are much more fun and easy to remember in a short amount of time. The message given by the parodies will be much more powerful than that written by a news story. Why don't the traditional media regard these parodies as news content? As you can see, there is a wide gap in perspectives between readers and the traditional media.

Journalists working for the traditional media had similar reactions. They were mostly, "is this news?" or "this kind of thing should go on the bulletin board." However, the distinction between news and bulletin boards is meaningless in the era of social networks. Readers regard traditional news as part of the content, not something they desire or should follow. What they pursue is fun and value. It should be fun and have a message in it. The form can be anything. Social network users consume not traditional news but fun and valuable content.

# 4. Transition to Social Media

## Anyone can see, hear, and do news

Journalists working at a traditional media company might get upset or intimidated by this chapter. Some content may sound unacceptable. However, from the news consumers' point of view, this will be a change they've longed for. Now, an individual will be able to play as the media. The existing news providers are standing on the opposite of the new consumers of the news. It will plunder the news providers, and the news consumers will gain a new status. From the plundered side, it is risky to stay the course. The painful choice is up to the plundered.

## Status of a journalist in the era of social networks

Journalists' biggest asset is their authority. If someone denied them this authority, it would be unacceptable for them. However, the paradigm shift that social networks brought along is making them give up on the authority. Are you a journalist? Take a deep breath and brace yourself for what is coming. If you close the book here, your chance to change will end here, too.

Journalism cannot be a professional occupation anymore. You may say, "What in the world are you talking about?" if you are in the media industry. However, in the era of social networks, journalists cannot boast of their specialties anymore.

A journalist writes fact-based, impartial news. To check facts, they try hard. Individually, and as a team from time to time, they work hard to find proofs to back up the truth. However, researches by an individual or a group of several reporters have limits. Moreover, it is harder to provide trustworthy news in this sense. Impartiality or fairness mostly depends on the media company's political identity and directions. An individual reporter's beliefs are not a priority to the media company.

A journalist has the expertise, and some have their specialties in specific fields. However, most of them experience team shifting from politics to economy, to culture, and the social desk. Even if a journalist is lucky enough to build some expertise in one field, his or her knowledge falls short of experts in the field. Experts in various fields exist outside the media, but they do not have direct access to the media. If they can use the media directly, professional journalists will lose competence.

A journalist writes stories well and is mostly well-trained. Cub reporters who passed the media company's job tests and interviews get hard training on writing. While covering their beats, they repeatedly write stories every day to sharpen their writing skills. However, many people outside the media write well. Moreover, they keep changing the story forms and styles in traditional media.

The reason journalists have had privilege was that they belong to newspaper or broadcasting companies. In the same sense, people who have insights, expertise, and excellent writing skills had no chance to play the role of a journalist just because they had no media.

It took an astronomical amount of capital to produce, publish, and distribute news. To publish newspapers, we need rotary press machines worth millions of dollars. To secure distribution channels, it requires vast capital. The broadcasting expenses are much higher. To run a broadcasting station, you should spend a much higher cost for equipment than to run a newspaper company. The state manages frequencies for broadcasting. It is impossible to broadcast without state approval. These reasons made media companies a rarity.

## Coming of the internet and crisis in news media

However, things are different now because of the internet. Anyone can produce, publish, and distribute news while spending almost nothing. The astronomical cost of publication and distribution dropped to zero. With a computer connected to the internet, anyone can produce news, publish it, and distribute it.

This change led to the rarity of media companies to disappear. Many experts and ordinary people are now able to write stories and publish them online without going through certain media. They prefer news written or recommended by their online neighbors and friends, rather than the news provided by the traditional media. It is a new trend created in the era of social networks.

The breakdown of this rarity directly influences the status of a journalist. The definition of a journalist was based on scarcity and incomplete. The expertise, regarded as something owned only by journalists, is not there. With the collapse of media rarity, the authority of journalists also collapsed.

Around the globe, media companies are screaming out. Beckett described this in his book *SuperMedia*: "Help, help, who will save us?" Then, should the media industry all die after all? Fortunately, no, as long as they are willing to change. Change what? Is change possible? Let's talk about this, though you might get upset. Once the media and journalists come out of their shells, they will come to an aha moment. Surprisingly, social networks will give entirely new, different opportunities and growth possibilities to the media.

# A fierce battle for real-time news

The first competitiveness of Internet-based newspapers was "real-time news." They reported the news immediately after the news broke. In the era of print media, the media gathered news articles for a day and set the deadline at a particular time. The newspaper printing system has been maintained for over 100 years. Then suddenly, real-time media companies appeared. Without a deadline, they produced stories all day long and reported them immediately online, which was an innovative approach.

# Real-time news service of internet newspapers

In Korea, Internet newspapers opened in 1999 to cover real-time news. They included OhMyNews, MoneyToday and iNews 24. As they did not have a deadline, they exposed the news immediately after the news broke. It was an innovative news service that no one else provided. Internet newspapers opened a new chapter for real-time news service.

Of course, existing newspapers and broadcasting companies had their websites, too. Joongang Ilbo's joins.com opened their newspapers on the website for the first time in March 1995. Korea's big dailies such as Chosun

Ilbo and Donga Ilbo did it as well, and most other dailies followed suit. Internet newspapers were three or four years faster in providing real-time news than the major newspapers in this trend.

However, internet newspapers run by media companies were just a complementary medium. After the first edition of the newspaper was confirmed, they copied the stories from the paper and put them online. Thus, it was rare to see an exclusive story on the internet first. When urgent news came out, they just put wire stories from the state-run wire service Yonhap News on the internet.

## The emergence of MoneyToday

MoneyToday, which specialized in stock news, emerged as a successful model of an online newspaper. Its entry into the Korean media industry marked a milestone in real-time news history. The news service opened in September 1999, and it was an unprecedented, successful case. It started as an online media and grew into a multi-functioning media company. It reached the break-even point only by online content, which was very rare in the media industry.

The first-phase strategy of MoneyToday was "focus." Insiders called it a "one-point breakthrough." The company wanted to focus on only one point and open a market there. MoneyToday focused solely on the news about listed companies in real time. While the stock market was open, the online company put all efforts into uploading news stories coming from listed companies. If the company could prove its influence on the stock market, it could enter into other news markets.

The strategy went successful. After MoneyToday wrote about a particular listed company, the stock price of the company moved along with the story, in real-time. If the content was positive, the stock price moved in red, and sometimes it peaked. If it was negative, the stock price moved the opposite in black.

MoneyToday developed a service to quicken the speed of news delivery. Other news sites started copying. The battle was fierce. To distinguish from the latecomers, MoneyToday had to develop a new service.

# News Quicker

Developers at MoneyToday made a tool called "News Quicker" to break news delivery. Internet users then called it "sticker." If you open the whole page of MoneyToday, you cannot see it while you work on other sites. However, the essence of MoneyToday's news service was "real-time." While you were working on other things, you had to see MoneyToday's news. So, the developers made the webpage a long bar. If you put it on top or bottom of the screen, you instantly know whenever news comes to you. When urgent news came out, a red light blinked, or an alarm rang.

The provision of News Quicker boosted MoneyToday's media power in terms of stocks. The movement of stock prices, along with the news content, became clear. With a stronger influence on the market, day traders started to send complaints. They said the news on News Quicker had 1 or 2 seconds of difference depending on the user. While day-trading investors were trading stocks, it was a big problem if the news was not delivered at the same time.

Day-traders look at multiple computers at the same time and trade stocks in a matter of seconds. One of the day traders opened News Quicker in two different PCs. Then, there was a time difference between the two when the breaking news came in. The day trader wrote an inquiry on MoneyToday's online bulletin board. Other readers, who saw the bulletin, got suspicious about whether someone might be trying to profit from that time difference.

MoneyToday's influence on stock prices was enormous then. If a news story about a stock was out, the stock price had a wild fluctuation. Therefore, 1 or 2 seconds of time difference was a big problem, considering the sensitivity of stock prices. Readers started to question whether someone was trying to gain profits from the time difference. It was a serious risk for MoneyToday.

The problem was the structure of the server system which produced, stored, and sent the news. The old system had about ten web servers in front and a database server containing the news content at the back. Whenever a reporter sends a story, the desk editor decides whether to expose the article. The system stored the confirmed stories in the backend database server, and the database server instantly sends the story to 10 web servers.

The issue occurred here. The system connected readers' PCs to 10 separate web servers. According to the server they linked, there should be a time difference that might happen even if it is very short. Sometimes it took nearly a second. A few readers raised issues that the time difference might result in unfair capital gain.

MoneyToday restructured the server system to solve this problem. The system redirected and stored all the news content created in the recent 24 hours to the system cache memory of the web servers instead of the backend database. It was to remove the time difference among the web servers.

## Real-time internet newspapers become old media

MoneyToday's focus on stock news enhanced the company's power in the stock market. Thanks to the market power of MoneyToday, the news it published became "news that earn[ed] money." In particular, it was essential for securities companies to subscribe to MoneyToday. MoneyToday sold news to websites of securities firms, major portal sites, and finance-related sites. In just one year after the news service launch, more than 50 websites purchased MoneyToday's news in the latter part of 2000.

Then, MoneyToday faced another battle, a battle with existing media companies. Yonhap News, the biggest news wire service in Korea, worried that MoneyToday seriously penetrated its market, especially regarding financial news. To prevent MoneyToday from eroding the market share, Yonhap News created a separate organization, joins.com, and invested a large amount of money in it. Then, joins.com was in the game, too. Joins.com exposed stories in the economy, finance, stocks and related areas on the website first before they were published in the Joongang Ilbo newspaper.

In this fierce battle, MoneyToday defeated Yonhap News and joins.com. In less than one year after challenging MoneyToday, the two companies concluded that they could not win in the game of real-time news service. The reason was that both companies were far from producing news 24 hours a day.

In Joongang Ilbo, the newsroom collects stories at a deadline once a day. The problem is that reporters there tend to write stories by the deadline. To change the habit of writing to make stories all day long and send them in real time was almost impossible. In other words, although the company prepared the technical system, they could not produce the content fast enough.

Yonhap News was confident in its real-time news service because it is a newswire service company. However, the reality turned the other way. The customers of Yonhap News were not readers but newspapers and broadcasters. These customers had deadlines; they were either morning papers or afternoon papers. Broadcasting companies also had deadlines for the main news. Thus, reporters at Yonhap News were far from achieving real-time reporting as well. They were used to writing stories in the time frame of deadlines according to the deadlines of morning and afternoon newspapers. In the end, Yonhap News could not catch up with MoneyToday.

I worked as Chief Information Officer of MoneyToday, managing the company's internet service. I was confident that Yonhap and joins.com's trial would fail because it was not a matter of technology but work culture. At MoneyToday, the company trained reporters to be "real-time reporters" who were obliged to write stories 24 hours a day. It was a must for them. However, for existing offline reporters, demanding this system was impossible.

With time, however, MoneyToday's competitiveness has been eroded. 2009 marked ten years since internet newspapers appeared in the market. In March 2009, there were 1,399 registered internet newspapers. By page view, MoneyToday ranked No. 1 among economic news media, but its status was not safe. Maeil Business News Korea had enhanced breaking news services as fast as MoneyToday. Another player, Asia Business Daily, had once beaten MoneyToday in urgent economic news. Other media companies were able to build a culture to produce news 24 hours a day during the ten years. The real-time news service became a "red ocean" where competition is fierce.

## Whether it is "social media" or not

Are you still preoccupied with the term "new media?" New media has become old already. Whether they are printed in newspapers or posted on the Internet, there is not much difference. They're all old media. Internet newspapers, which once competed with real-time news service, have lost their competitive edge. Existing media are providing real-time news as well. Even magazine sites provide real-time news.

The speedy reporting of breaking news is nothing new now. The comments under an online story were innovative ten years ago because readers couldn't express opinions or criticism on the article without the internet. However, all this has become an "old model." Why? Because everyone does it. So, it's not "new media" anymore.

## It is "social" now

While social networks are changing the media paradigm, discussing whether it is new media or not is meaningless. Now, it's whether you are social media or not. It is time that you have to think about how to add news services on social networks and how to synchronize the media with social networks. To do this, you should re-define all elements and process of news production. You should change the concept and form of news, reporter's function and role, newsroom's structure, tasks, and the characters and styles of advertisement. Social networks fundamentally changed the relationship between the media and readers, and the behaviors of readers towards news.

## Oligopoly collapses

The media was a capital-intensive industry. When newspapers and broadcasting companies dominated the market, establishing a newspaper or a broadcaster needed an astronomical amount of money. Newspaper companies needed lots of money to purchase rotary press machines, hire reporters, and secure distribution networks. Newspapers had to buy or rent many real estates to secure distribution bases, in addition to spending on producing and printing news.

Broadcasting companies had a higher barrier to market entry. To equip with broadcasting machines took a massive amount of money. It takes human resources and high cost to produce content for a broadcaster, which is incomparable to newspaper production. Besides, broadcasting companies needed government approval to secure channels. Radio broadcast frequencies and TV station channels were oligopolistic.

The advent of the internet began to dismantle the oligopolistic media industry. The impact hit news production first. Anyone who had a PC could write articles on a word processor and edit them. As PCs gained access to the Internet, anyone was able to put the articles on the World Wide Web. This phenomenon went beyond the individual level. With PCs connected to the Internet, people could publish online newspapers with small capital. Then, online papers mushroomed here and there, armed with the technology of real-time news service.

## Social networks take over portal news

However, internet newspapers became even more oligopolistic due to the portal-centered online system. Huge portals—frequented by a majority of internet users—became hubs where news stories produced by online papers were gathered and distributed. Whether an internet newspaper survived or not depended on whether large portals such as Naver or Daum put their stories on the portal's main page or not.

Portals aggregated news articles produced by internet newspapers in one place. The issue of selecting news to publish on a selected position on the portal's page was meant to emerge. In the end, the news service of portals was just another internet newspaper service in a bigger frame.

Social networks enabled readers to bypass portals to find news. On social networks, the news is recommended by friends who have similar interests. The news is carefully adjusted according to your preferences, not just shoved together by internet newspapers or portals. You can choose from among the news you read and recommend it to your friends only by clicking it once.

Social networks solved the inconvenient communication problem that internet newspapers and portal services had. The news was not confined to media companies anymore. Anyone could write a news story and upload it on social networks so that others who found it interesting could share it, automatically creating the news production and distribution channels. The news production and distribution went into the hands of individuals, which resulted in the dismantling of the oligopolistic media market.

The rarity of news-producing human resources was also gone. Journalists who worked for media companies had to brace themselves for what was coming. They have wake up and smell the coffee. There are many more good writers out there than those in the newsroom. Experts exist outside of the newsroom. They want to have their voices and promote themselves. They had great difficulty in getting access to the media. Even if they could access, they had to go through many layers, including the interest of a journalist, the checks of an editor, and the media company's political preferences. It was another matter whether the reported news will spread wide enough and whether the media company had enough influential power to do so. Then, in the era of social networks, those layers became meaningless.

## Inverted pyramid becomes outdated

It is not easy to have professional skills as a journalist. To become a competent journalist, he or she should be able to catch news-worthy issues and write stories in the form of an "inverted pyramid" to prioritize the information. Unfortunately, these core skills do not work in the era of social networks.

## New styles of news on social networks

The scope of reportage, also known as "coverage," of the traditional media is very narrow while the interest of people is vast and diverse. The scope of issues reporters can choose from a newsroom is very limited. To make matters worse, the number of reporters is going down with the decline of the media industry, which makes the coverage even narrower. Social networks have the natural function of creating issues. Many users create opinions through mutual interactions. The interest of people has centered on their lives, and various issues appear in their daily lives. People freely express their opinions on social networks and share them with friends who have similar interests. The function of shaping issues went from a small number of reporters to several networked individuals.

The structure of an inverted pyramid, regarded as an unbreakable rule among reporters, should be reconsidered. On the internet, liberal stories with various writing styles float around. Internet users are more comfortable with liberal writing styles in comments, entries on an online cafe, and blogs. It is hard to see a story written in an inverted pyramid. Stories with texts only are considered boring. Internet users mix pictures, animation, video, and cartoons. Their choice of words is quite different from that in news stories produced by newspapers. Their storytelling method is entirely different from that of newspapers.

Now, we have to think about how the current format of writing styles in newspapers and broadcasting companies was created in the first place. Did readers want the inverted pyramid? Did readers like the format? It was because the format was the most efficient way to deliver news on limited space of a paper or in a limited broadcasting time. It was the best way to produce as much news as possible in the quickest way, created and defined by the media. Readers, who suffered an absolute shortage of news supply, had to accept what the media created.

## Content value goes beyond format

The most significant assets of the Internet as a medium are that it is "real-time" and has "limitless space." It does not matter how long or how short a story is. The internet accepts those stories as they are. If the story is interesting, it is read by many, no matter how long it is. Even if it is just a few sentences or a simple picture, it will be consumed by readers again and again. There is no rule. Readers who are used to social networks and the internet do not think the format is important. It is whether the content is interesting to read or valuable. Now, journalists should find a new role to play.

In the end, it will be meaningless to write a fully-formatted story. Reporters' exclusive skills are almost useless nowadays. In the news market, oligopolistic human resources do not exist anymore. Social networks have created an ecology where anyone can tell their stories in their own ways and share them.

## Starting from scratch

The oligopolistic system the media industry had is forever gone now. There is no entry barrier, no expertise in human resources, and no need for machines, platforms, and distribution channels. The media is now in the infinite market competition against people. Traditional media has nothing special. It will be tremendously hard for the media to accept this reality and get adjusted.

## Grab new opportunities on social networks

It is a bitter reality for traditional media. What's more shocking is that they lost their name value as well. Whether it is Chosun Ilbo, Joongang, Donga or new internet newspapers, their brands do not matter on social networks. Readers do not approach an individual story by looking at the media company's name. They scan the headlines recommended by their friends on social networks and click them only when they're interested. If the content is satisfying enough, they share it with other friends. If not, they close the browser. During this process, they are not interested in which media company published that story. Their standard of selecting news is whether they are interested or their friends recommended it. No news consumer looks for the title of the media company.

A media company might be small or large, old or new, or traditional or emerging. A media company can attract newsreaders' attention as long as the news content is fun and valuable. Therefore, social networks offer the same opportunity to every media. All media stood at the starting line from scratch. The traditional media should stand by the starting line if they understood what was going on. Existing small media companies, local newspapers, and internet newspapers are given the same opportunity as well. Social networks dismantled the old oligopolistic system and gave equal opportunity to all the media. The challenge is to precisely understand news consumers' behavior and create news service that fits in the era of social networks.

# 5. News media faces a sea change

## Media ownership is being open to individuals

The boundary of the media blurred. It is not talking about the boundaries of newspapers, broadcasting companies, and internet media. What we are talking about is whether it is media or not. In other words, social individuals who were not used to be media are now taking up the role of the media. Social individuals refer to institutions, government bodies, and individuals.

Everybody will become media. Everyone's desire to do so is getting stronger because anybody can write news and send it to readers.

Twitter defined itself as "news media." Twitter's vice president Kevin Thau in 2010 said Twitter is not a "social network" but a "news network." He said, "Twitter is changing the very nature of news." He also declared that it would "allow everyday users to become journalists themselves by providing them with a simple mechanism to breaking news."

Then, Twitter changed the message in the tweet window from "What are you doing?" to "What's happening?" It means Twitter expects you to write news, not daily stories. In other words, every tweet on Timeline is news. It is the same with Facebook. The very nature of news has been shaken.

For first-time users of Facebook, "News Feed" can be somewhat confusing. In "News Feed," you expect to receive news, but you will find that posts from your friends will appear one after another. First-time Facebook users would have expected news articles from traditional media. Of course, you can be friends with traditional media. However, all the postings either from the media or your friends are "news."

Facebook's News Feed provides all the news of all the people who connected as friends. They are "social news," a new concept of news on social networks. We are living in it now. For example, someone witnesses a car accident on the way to work in the morning. At work, he or she will talk about this to coworkers. Even after work, the accident probably will be an outstanding topic for dinner with family. Our nature wants to talk about meaningful thing repeatedly.

How about on social networks? Smart readers armed with Facebook or Twitter-linked smartphones take out their phones from a pocket when they witness a car accident. They can take pictures, post them on Twitter or Facebook to talk about the accident to their friends. They are not self-conscious about their news production. However, from the traditional media's view, they can be news stories, live news reports from incident scenes and scoops.

## Twitter captures a photo of Haeundae fire scene

On Oct 1, 2010, a fire broke at a high-rise apartment building in Haeundae's Marine City, Busan, southern Korea. It was a massive fire, and one Twitter user took the first picture of the burning fire immediately after the ignition. It is almost impossible for professional photographers to take an ignition fire because when they usually get to the scene, they take either black smokes or a wide spread of fire. However, Twitter allowed users to take the first fire immediately after the ignition.

Major daily newspapers in Korea, including Chosun Ilbo, Maeil Business Daily, and Korea Business Daily, printed the picture of the Haeundae fire scene taken by Twitter user @swsong10 as a heading image as shown at right(*photo by @swsong10 / Tweeter*). The flame was dramatically going upward to the top of the building in the photo. At the very moment when the fire broke, there was a Twitter user with a smartphone. He took a picture of the scene and posted it on Twitter. It is why he wanted to talk about the scene to his friends on Twitter.

 In the traditional media environment, a picture taker would have called media companies to send the picture. However, smart readers can talk about it to friends on social networks. While smart readers easily share conversations, media companies will regard such a picture as a hot scoop.

It is almost zero possibility that a photojournalist can take such right-on-the-spot picture. At the moment of the fire, photographers have to be near the incident scene with his camera.

However, there were two other Twitter pictures taken near the Haeundae scene. Among them, the photo by @swsong10 had the most vigorous intensity and the right angle.

Three Twitter pictures of the fire scene explain well that how much "social news" phenomenon is quickly spreading. Smart readers are overwhelmingly becoming superior to traditional news media in terms of the scope of the news coverage and the intensity of the report.

## Social news on KTX failure gets faster than internal report

On March 20, 2011, Korea's high-speed train KTX suddenly stopped inside a tunnel, just in 10 minutes after leaving Busan Station at noon. An announcement came out saying "the train will go back to Busan due to failure in the operating system" at 12:39. This news was

up on social news media Wikitree by one passenger who was in the first-

class car. The passenger also posted a photo of an inside picture of KTX passenger car, with the texts of the announcement.

This news quickly spread on Twitter. Twitter users reacted with many comments such as "Oh, I can see lots of KTX failures these days," "I am humiliated with Korea's KTX," and "I hope the trouble gets fixed as soon as possible." Even though it was Sunday, the number of Twitter accounts reached by this news surpassed 600,000.

The news on Twitter was reported as "breaking news" on TV news programs. It was exactly one hour after the Twitter news broke that TV stations began reporting the KTX failure. Surprisingly, before the KTX failure was internally reported to the train operator KORAIL's headquarters, Twitter users already shared what happened. Twitter's news breaking and propagation power are formidable, especially in incidents and accidents.

The influence of social networks on media is straightforward and fundamental. Anyone can be a journalist and can cover any topic. Every new thing to me become news to others. The distinction between news consumers and news producers becomes meaningless. Now, they should be all called "news participants." There is no pure news reader or news consumer. At the same time, there is no pure news producer either. All produce and consume news as "news participants."

# Twitter calms controversy over human rights infringement after "bra undressing" of woman

What news participants want is quite different from news consumers in the past. They want to see themselves raw news sources untouched. It is a phenomenal change created in the social media environment. It is the most significant change I have experienced, as the operator of social news service provider Wikitree.

For example, social networks in Korea were heated over a policeman's request for a female college student to undress her bra during the interrogation of her involvement in demonstrations for reduction of tuition in June 2011. While news reports criticizing the police dominated the online news, a clarification statement on Gwangjin Police Station's Twitter account was explosively retweeted and instantly soothed the controversy.

Under the name of the police chief, the statement made the point that bras were defined as dangerous objects as they can be used in suicide attempts, while the interrogated student was seen likely to attempt any self-injury or suicide. It also explained that the student was told to take off her bra herself, and the police made sure she was not embarrassed.

The statement refuted criticism, one by one, in detail. What matters here was whether the statement was fact-based and sincere. If the statement were not based on facts or not honest, it would have made the situation worse. Wikitree put up the statement as a whole on its website and sent it on Twitter. Thanks to the tweet that went viral, controversies over human rights infringement of the woman abated soon.

## I don't want news; I want the whole statement

 We have to pay attention here. News participants want to directly hear from news sources, without any filter. They already have access to raw materials and directly comment on them because they know their messages can be spread on others on social media. Rather than following journalists' judgment, they try to share their view. It is a new trend.

"One to many" conversation structure of social networks allows a powerful collective intelligence. The collective intelligence can help find the truth of an incident and flip election results sometimes.

During the process, the traditional media is just another news participants. Individual users regard themselves as "peers" of journalists. They want to see news raw materials intact, rather than edited, re-arranged, and sometimes, biased stories written by journalists.

 There are many other cases where social network users enthusiastically responded to "full text" of statements. If a story is attached with a full text, the traffic of the story shoots up and the number of Twitter RTs skyrockets. Companies, institutions, government bodies, and individuals, who were not categorized as media before, started to open their news channels. They include Samsung Electronics' SMNR and Foreign Ministry's MOFAT Story.

# Important news comes to readers

Several years ago, Don Tapscott's book "*Wikinomics*" became an inspiration for me. The book and Clay Shirky's "*Here Comes Everybody*" gave me an excellent insight into how news media will change in the near future. Tapscott released another book, "*Macrowikinomics*." He devoted a whole chapter to talk about news media. The title of the chapter is "The Demise of the Newspaper and the Rise of the New News."

Even if newspapers threaten not to deliver papers unless readers pay for news, important news will come to readers without any problem, on the internet or social networks, for free. Whether it is a piece of important news or not, the decision is up to readers. It means readers will not be coerced to follow the values of the news that were pre-set by media companies. Even if a news media repeatedly says it has an exclusive story, the story will lose value unless readers regard it as important.

It is happening quite frequently now. On February 15, 2011, Korea's state-run TV station KBS reported scenes of the late North Korean former leader Kim Jong-il's second son Jong-chul enjoying the concert of Eric Clapton in Singapore. A news anchor, before the news report, said the upcoming KBS news would be "a huge scoop."

After they aired the report, KBS faced adverse reactions and criticism from Twitter users. They were upset that Kim Jong-chul's playtime should not be top headline news while South Korea suffered foot-and-mouth disease of kettles across the nation.

# Digital on the outside, analog on the inside

Everybody says we live in a digital era. No one can deny it. Then, is our news digital? No, I definitely say.

Newspapers still make news on papers. Broadcasting companies do so on TV screens. Some will say they make "digital" news on their websites. I would say it is true only on the outside.

Newspapers produce news that will be printed out on papers. Broadcasting companies make news to air it on TV. Then, they put HTML or XML tags on these news reports and hang them on the internet homepages. Because the news reports are on the internet, they call this digital. However, these news reports have put on digital code, but they are still analog inside.

I urge them to "throw away papers." Why do they find it natural to assume that they will write news on paper? It is a habit, a tradition, and a strong stereotype.

Let's throw away papers. When we write news, let's assume we write on digital papers. Digital stories have different elements or components that were not handled by traditional media. Elements of news stories in the old days were texts, pictures, and illustration cuts. In broadcasting, they included videos and audio files.

What are the elements of digital stories? They include talking photos, "mapping" to show the location on the map, video clips, polls, augmented reality, and QR codes. News stories can include background music and offer a slideshow of many pictures. Even "data journalism" exists to show data in multi-dimensional graphics.

## Please forget about the papers!

News stories become digital if we consider those elements before the production of news. Formats of digital news can change again depending on distribution channels -- web pages, smartphones, tablet PCs, and smart TVs. News stories for papers are just one of them, not the initial news stories to be distributed to other channels. So I urge you to "forget about papers."

News consumers have already changed their consumption behavior to digital. At least they are moving fast to digital. An increasing number of people are moving to smartphones from newspapers to read the news. As of November 2011, the number of smartphone users hit 20 million in South Korea. The statistics symbolize sea change in news consumer behavior. It is sporadic to see a subway commuter reading a newspaper now. Do you still want to hold on to papers?

We do not use smartphones to see texts and photos. We expect lively digital stories that are convenient and easy to read with various elements that give life to the stories. In there, there can be astronomical added values and usefulness. Shift your mindset and make news stories on smartphones instead of papers.

We do not have to ask ourselves if we are writing digital news. Are you writing news that fits smartphone screens? Are you using various smart elements properly? If you say no, forget about papers immediately!

News consumers have already left. New readers will not come to that place. Let's move the news target. Why do you still expect readers to remain there? If you move the target, you should also move the aiming point. Digital news does not refer to the news on the internet. Please forget about papers and write digital stories.

## Broadcasting companies keep locking content

Once I was invited to a broadcasting company to give a lecture about social networks and news media. After the lecture, one news program PD asked me how to "raise TV ratings using social networking services (SNS)." Below is what I said.

"It is deplorable that broadcasting companies want many people to watch their TV programs while they have locked their content. To raise viewer ratings, open them up."

Korean broadcasting companies have tightly locked content of programs. They just put a website of programs. Unless viewers install each different video players of different broadcasting companies, they cannot watch the content. If they want to watch a past episode, they have to sign up and log in. There are too many barriers to watch a past episode. Even if viewers did all the required things to watch an episode, they could not share it on to other sites.

Understandably, broadcasting companies want to keep their intellectual property rights because their programs cost much money and many people's efforts. However, such a mindset is just a stereotype.

In "social-mobile era" where social networking services meet mobile, TV programs should be shared on social media. "Sharing" is "copying." On a mobile environment, the content should be put on open platforms like

"YouTube" or "Vimeo" so that it can be available on all kinds of mobile devices.

Let's take the example of YouTube. U.S. broadcasting companies do not regard YouTube as a competitor but a useful channel to promote themselves. ABC has a YouTube channel under @ABCnews, CNN with @CNN and Fox with @FoxTV. They promote their news programs and other TV programs on YouTube channels. Some upload their entire news program on it, and some others use it to spread trailers. They are quite the opposite to their Korean counterparts who are anxious to check if someone else might "steal" their content and hang it up on YouTube.

## Al Jazeera hits jackpot after opening up

Opening up will create opportunities for broadcasters. Arabic broadcaster Al Jazeera took "open policy," when the Egyptian Mubarak authorities banned the internet and social networking sites in 2011.

Al Jazeera put photos of demonstration scenes in Egypt, taken by their journalists, on Flikr, a social networking photo site, under the account name of @AljazeeraEnglish. They opened the copyrights of the photos and allowed them to be shared. The broadcaster used the Creative Commons License on the shared photos and users could use the photos any time, as long as they credit them and not make changes to the originals. At the same time, they put 24-hour live news reports on demonstrations in Egypt on YouTube under @AljazeeraEnglish in real-time.

The photos and videos of the scenes in Egypt spread across the globe on social networks. Al Jazeera was the only channel to receive the latest updates on Egyptian demonstrations even when the internet was banned. Since then, people's awareness of Al Jazeera shot up. Then, in the U.S., a civil campaign started to help Al Jazeera English to be included in U.S. cable channels. Without any cost, Al Jazeera English could join the U.S. cable channels. It is the power of "opening up."

Let's go back to the Q&A session during my lecture and think about the TV producer who asked how to raise program viewer ratings. Let's say the producer made a preview of the program to boost the viewer ratings. They should insert the preview between TV commercials they are airing between programs. There is no way to measure precisely how many viewers actually saw the preview. Only those who kept the TV set on at that right time could see the preview. Moreover, the broadcaster had to give up ad revenue that they can have in case they had not made the preview.

What if the broadcaster opens the content of the preview on YouTube? And what if they allow anyone to share it on social networks like Twitter and Facebook? How about making a fun video clip showing the highlights of the program instead of a predictable, lame preview? How about having conversations about the fun preview with viewers on social networks? We don't even have to discuss the result.

The solution is "opening up." It is not only about broadcasters. It applies to newspapers, magazines and all kinds of news media. News media in the social-mobile news era should open up. The more they open, the more opportunities will come.

## Conservative media's attack on Twitter

"Twitter is a deadly weapon for 'verbal terrorism.'" (Chosun Ilbo)

"SNS grows on rough words...Not a communication space but a tool of witch-hunting'" (Donga Ilbo)

These are expressions about Twitter written by the conservative newspapers published in November 2011. On Chosun Ilbo, it was the title of the editorial. On Donga Ilbo, it was the title of a box story. Donga Ilbo even used an illustration of Twitter's logo bluebird, which was carrying daggers on both wings like an assassin.

The by-election of Seoul Mayor in 2011 proved that social networks, including Twitter, had a strong influence. When the issue of the free trade agreement between Korea and the U.S divided Koreans pro and cons, a majority of Korean Twitter users were opposing the FTA. Then, Chosun and Donga Ilbo expressed "worries" over Twitter. Unfortunately, they showed those worries in "spiteful language."

Twitter users turned sarcastic about the two vernaculars' attacks on Twitter. Here are some notable mentions on Twitter; "From the viewpoint of Chosun

Ilbo's right-sided and biased editorial tendency, Twitter can be seen 'terroristic.' However, a majority of Korean people share the right information through two-way communication;" "Twitter is the only thing Cho Joong Dong (Chosun, Joongang and Donga Ilbo) is afraid of." The two newspapers' spiteful words returned to them like a boomerang.

Twitter offers space for communication. At the same time, it is media. For the traditional media, it is a distribution channel as well as space for communication. Twitter users are someone you have conversations with as well as active readers of your news.

In the past, newspaper readers could not spread their opinions to other readers and keep them recorded in the media. Newspapers' editorials and news articles were sent one-way to readers and readers regarded them as "majority's opinions." Even if they had opposite opinions, they had to share them only with friends and family, not the entire people out there.

Social networks made the situation very different. So many readers on social networks talk to each other in real-time, bypassing the media. Many people exchange reactions to the particular news. The responses are all recorded on social networks and exposed to everyone. At the same time, the media and the news get instant judgment and evaluations from social network users. Now, people trust more in evaluations by many than in the media.

What kind of efforts did the traditional media make to get adjusted to new media like Twitter? The Twitter users did not welcome Korea's leading newspapers, including Chosun, Joongang, and Donga Ilbo. Digital media bloter.net conducted "media Twitter index analysis" in September 2011. Chosun Ilbo ranked 4th in quotation rate, 9th in exposure rate, and 10th in sustaining power on Twitter. However, in the number of exposures per story and propagation power of a story, it could make it within 20th. Donga Ilbo ranked 17th in quotation rate and 13th in the number of exposures per story. In the rest of the categories, it couldn't rank within 20th.

However, during the survey, Chosun Ilbo was third and Donga Ilbo, 7th, in the number of stories put up on Twitter. Why couldn't they rank high although they sent out so many stories on Twitter?

I'm not trying to show sarcasm here. I want to make a point that the traditional media should look back on how much effort they made to enhance communication on Twitter. If they feel frustrated and upset by Twitter users' rejection to be fed with one-way communication, the situation will get worse.

The communication on Twitter is horizontal and sentimental. If a media tries to boast its authority, it will be rejected or criticized. Twitter users are active readers. The media which pour out bitter sarcasm on readers will lose readership in the end.

# 6. Devices for social-mobile News

## News market moves on to "social-mobile news"

With a speedy distribution of mobile devices with high performance and low price, the news market is moving fast to mobile. The market moved from newspapers and magazines to broadcasting and the internet. Recently it moved to social networks and is moving to a new market where social networks and mobile services are combined. Now it is the era of "social-mobile news."

Mobile devices made social networks more popular. The steep increase in the number of Facebook and Twitter users resulted from the popularity of iPhones. With the spread of iPhones, Twitter and Facebook experienced explosive growth. Smartphones like the iPhone and social networks are a fabulous match. It is almost impossible not to know Twitter if you're an iPhone user.

Smartphones boosted the number of social network users and the frequency of social network usage. Smartphones offered all-time internet access, mobility, easy multimedia tools, and high performance at reasonable prices. They provided real-time access, communication with many others, content verification by collaboration, easy exchange of multimedia, and openness that anyone can use. With traits of smartphones and social networks combined, the social-mobile news market has a significant change.

In the era of social-mobile news, PCs, smartphones, tablet PCs, and smart TVs should be looked at again. They are "smart devices." From the perspective of news readers or news producers, we have to think about what characteristics they can offer. If you understand them well, you can realize which device fits which format. It is the essence of social-mobile news service.

## Smart readers look for "ambiance"

If we carefully look how people use desktop PCs and smart devices when they read news, we can find out how to produce news and shape the form of news according to the characteristics of those devices. Now the news market's demand side will be led by "smart readers" who use smart devices as well as desktop PCs.

Smart readers do not hold on to a single device. To read the news, they would not look for newspapers or turn on the internet in front of a desktop. They naturally scan and choose news at a convenient time and place, using the most convenient device available. It is called "ambiance." Smart devices exist around smart readers and offer "ambience" according to their respective functions.

Simple news consumers can enjoy "ambiance." They do not have to explain why they chose a particular device at a certain point. However, from the perspective of news providers, we have to know the exact reason why news consumers chose a specific device at a particular time. That way, we will not interfere with smart readers' ambiance, which is the basics of consuming and spreading the news.

## Desktop PC for smart devices and its secure status

A desktop PC is the most traditional device for news on social networks. No matter how many smartphones people used widely, even if an iPad is right next to you, also if you watch exciting entertainment and news programs on a smart TV, a desktop PC is still important to you. It has substantial merit as news device.

In terms of function, the PC can display the most various screens. Opening multiple windows on one monitor makes you check multiple sites at the same time. One window can be divided into several frames as well. A desktop PC's speed of the internet is much faster than mobile devices. It has better security than mobile ones. Thanks to high-speed broadband and plentiful storage, a desktop PC becomes a hub for mobile devices. PCs have even stronger status in the mobile environment.

From the aspect of user behavior, PCs offer a special status. Users sit at a desk to use a PC. It is essential to use a PC when working, writing, and researching. It requires high concentration. Users spend a long time working at a desktop.

In terms of performance, PCs are great. It has the most precise and fastest input devices, such as a keyboard and a mouse. It can install a graphics board, a tablet, and individual devices according to various purposes. There is no such useful device like a PC to process multimedia because of its ample storage and speedy CPU. We can connect it with a scanner, a camera, electronic instruments, and musical instruments.

## Magic of smartphones with mobility and sensing

The most substantial merit of a smartphone is that it is readily available within your reach whenever and wherever. In other words, it has "portability." On your palm, you can see it anywhere in a comfortable pose. You may be on a sofa, with a cup of coffee, on a bus or subway, and you may be waiting for food during lunch. Whenever you have a minute, you can take a glimpse at the smartphone.

A smartphone is a private device. It has an entirely private user environment. The screen is small and almost always viewed by one person, which makes the concentration level very high.

## The news comes to you

Readers do not have to find news now. In the era of social-mobile news, news comes to readers. Readers can put tags on a piece of news along with push functions on smart devices. On social networks, the news comes from links shared by your friends. You don't have to sit at the desk to read the news.

In the matter of schedule, you don't have to do that either. Morning papers are delivered in the early morning and evening news on TV usually starts at 9 p.m. It is "news by appointment." In the era of social-mobile news, the media and readers are all connected simultaneously. Smart readers find it natural to read news whenever they want to. The news by appointment is meaningless. People do not care if a morning paper arrived late, and 9 p.m. TV news program will lose its power. Broadcasting companies should produce news 24 hours a day, in real-time, so that readers can get the latest news on smart TVs or smartphones.

# Smart readers are news owners

In the era of social-mobile news, readers do not consume "packaged news." Smart readers do not wait at a certain time to read a morning newspaper or watch 9 p.m. news program. They have control over what to read and watch.

Smart readers also produce and distribute news thanks to affordable and high-performing smart devices. You don't need a pricey video camera and an editing machine to provide news for broadcasting, as long as you have a smartphone with HD imaging technology. You can edit the video using free, simple, and easy-to-use editing apps.

In storing and delivering news, there is no barrier. There are numbers platforms such as YouTube that store video clips for free. Delivery occurs on social networks. It is enough to put the news links on Facebook and Twitter. It is just a matter of time to make valuable or informative news spread on social networks. Readers can purely evaluate news regardless of the brand of the news media. Smart readers approach news, not by the brand of the media. As long as they're interested, they click on the news recommended by friends. If they like it, they share it with other friends.

Because the traditional media do not understand the behavior of smart readers and approach the news market in the old way, smart readers have turned their backs from them. Smart readers do not recognize the authority that the traditional media once thought they had. The oligopolistic media market got disintegrated entirely, and smart readers have taken new behaviors. Smart readers already know that they have the same status as a media with the traditional media on social networks.

# 7. Cross-Platform Reporting

## Remember CAR?

In 2000, Computer-Assisted Reporting (CAR) was a new trend in the media industry. It involved how to facilitate computers for news reporting. It was about searching data or materials on the internet, process data in spreadsheets, and write an article based on the processed data. It was also about directly communicating with news sources via emails when writing stories. Almost every university's communication department had courses on CAR.

Back then, it was rare a journalist used the internet, understood database, and communicated through emails. Journalism majors had to learn these skills in courses, and the media people had to be separately trained. Now, CAR is just common sense. It is quite silly to learn those skills. Even teenagers know how to do them. However, I remind you again that it was just 15 years ago when people needed specialized training for these simple skills.

## Multimedia platforms everywhere

More than ten years have passed. The CAR has been upgraded to multimedia. Newspapers now want to put video and audio in their news stories, mainly composed of texts and photos. Multimedia reporting is technologically possible, but related machines are pricey and difficult to use. It is hard for a single reporter to produce multimedia news.

## Who produces more fun news?

However, things have changed. The production equipment has come to your hands. A smartphone is enough for creating multimedia news. You can edit full-HD video with a flip camera. It is easy to use. You instantly know how to do it without going over the manual.

Storage for video is also limitless for free. Services such as YouTube, Vimeo, Livestream, and Ustream offer not just storage. They help you create a format so that your video can show up on any site on the internet. They give you an independent URL so you can spread your video anywhere, a source code to put it on a webpage, and connect it to social networks. That is why we call these sites "platforms."

There are not only video platforms but photo platforms like Flickr. Fotobabble is a platform where you can mix photos with audio. Animoto offers photo slideshow services. If you use platforms such as Polldaddy, SurveyMonkey, or Zoomerang, you can insert an instant survey into a news story. You can put a geographical location in the story if you use a map service such as Google Maps. You can air a live report on a smartphone.

## Smart readers are already used to platforms

We need to understand this very clearly; social readers are already used to the various platforms. They are enjoying content made with photos, videos, and parodies on blogs and postings on online communities. The traditional news format, a text-centered story with one or two photos, is just one part of many formats they encounter. Instead, the conventional news format makes smart readers bored and tired. Smart readers quickly lightly process news messages, precisely choosing necessary platforms.

In this, there is an opportunity. While other media companies stick to their old news format, you can find a new format that meets the needs of smart readers. The challenge is who will do it first.

The media should now engage in "Cross-Platform Reporting" or CPR. It is a skill to use various platforms, gather information for storytelling, and make a news out of them. Just as CAR does not require teamwork, CPR can and should be done individually.

## Why CPR?

There is another reason we need CPR. It can create profits. CPR is different from the old news format and more fun as well. Even if it is the same news topic, CPR allows a whole new different format.

Here is an important market principle. Same or similar news stories are put up on various media websites. Whether it is a newspaper or a broadcasting company, they show similar news stories here and there. The price of the news, as a product, goes down due to too many alternatives.

If there are too many alternatives, the price goes down to zero. However, the traditional media are trying to find a way how to provide paid news service, while the price of news has become zero. Even it is the same news from the same incident, the news presented in different ways can be distinctive. CPR enables this.

By using CPR, the delivery of the news content will be speedier, and the news will become more interesting to read and spread wider. Producers of news have to think who will change the mindset first.

Let's say an incident occurred at your sight. If you are a reporter, you will think you need to write an article. "Writing an article" comes from the mindset of corresponding texts. You would think, "If I write an article, the photographer will take the photo, and the editor will edit my story. What I have to do is to write an inverted pyramid article, and others will take care of the photos and videos because they are not my business."

## Do not write an article but build a story

To create CPR-based news on social-mobile media, the very first motive should change. Your intention to "write an article" should be changed to "building a story." To make the story most effective, you should think about whether to take pictures, or videos, or record voices and what part should write in texts, in a multitasking mode.

In some cases, a single photo can deliver a more precise and faster message than a news article. Some pictures can be edited with speech balloons and made like cartoons if that is the most effective way. A short, shaky, out-of-focus video clip can deliver everything, including the intensity of the incident. If this kind of situation is written in texts, the news might not spread at all. We should do away with "text-centered" mindsets. To find the most appropriate method and make use of the relevant platform is the essence of CPR.

CPR does not require high-quality video or sophisticated angles. It needs just a simple video clip which should not be longer than 1 minute. The CPR-purposed video clip is not a well-organized masterpiece. The short video clip should deliver a message in the most effective and fastest way.

We can use CPR for both features and straight news. For urgent news, its power is enormous. If it is urgent, it could be just several words in an audio file or a photo. A video clip can directly show the intensity of an incident. Its role is very different from that of the videos of the traditional broadcasting companies. Anyone can shot a video clip with a smartphone or a flip camera. The point is, we should do away with writing texts in breaking urgent news.

One more thing to say here is that people might think we have to use a mixture of several multimedia in one news article, such as texts, photos, and videos. Of course, we can. However, it is okay to use just one single media to do so, as long as the media effectively delivers a clear message. CPR does not mean mixing serval media but choose the most effective media and make use of the platform that can support the media. Doing this properly in a short amount of time can be the professional asset of news producers.

I suggest you remember how news articles looked in the past. Moreover, compare them to the ones described above. Compare their news formats. There is a considerable change. Success depends on who will grab the opportunity to change. The opportunity is open to everyone, not only to media companies. Here comes a new news market that social-mobile era has opened.

# 8. social-mobile News Distribution

## How smart readers consume news

In the era of social-mobile news, smart readers see three things when approaching news: interesting issue, recommendations by friends, and their location. If they open traditional media's websites, they have to pay too high opportunity cost. They have to choose news articles themselves and give up on other online news. To do so, they should reduce their time on social networks.

When they are on social networks, things change. They don't have to select one newspaper and still get access to numerous news in the conversations with friends. That news includes not only made by the media but independent content producers. The most credible thing is that their friends whom they trust recommend that news. They can reduce efforts to filter out unnecessary news. On social networks, all is simple. From the perspective of simple economics, it is clear to understand why smart readers consume news on social networks and do not find the titles of the media in the news.

## Understand news participation

Another important characteristic of social news consumer is their participation in news making. Smart readers do not merely consume news but have mindsets that they are always part of the news. The most popular form of engagement is evaluations on the news. On social networks, if they find it interesting or valuable, they recommend the news link to friends. This recommendation is the first evaluation of the news content.

On top of the recommendation, users often show their reactions while linking. On Twitter, they add a short mention while retweeting. It is an active engagement in the news. Proper storage of the comments, mentions, and feedbacks of the news will be a sound evaluation system.

The most active participants in the news are to raise opposite opinions when the news content is misleading. It is the process of gatekeeping by collective intelligence. Surprisingly, the gatekeeping occurs quite often. If the news is far from facts, smart readers raise questions immediately. The media's reputation on social networks depends on how it deals with issues raised by smart readers.

In many cases, smart readers also produce news content. Without being aware that they are telling the news, they share information. If the individual information is gathered in one place, it can be compelling news that overwhelms the traditional media. For example, when there is a storm coming or heavy rainfall, numerous Twitter users can take pictures and update what's happening. It will create a quick but enormous amount of news. On social networks, the number of news content already outnumbered the news produced by the media.

Moreover, smart readers only create but reproduce news-worthy issues. The size of the issue depends on the speed of other users' reactions and the scope of the dissemination. It is also very active participation in news production.

## Social networks are not portals

There is a big difference between social networks and portals. While many users communicate with other many users based on participation and mutual interactions on social networks, portals have a linear, one-to-many communication system. Portals are an aggregated online service, just as "portal" refers to a gate connected to many sites.

Reading online news on portals is not different from reading individual online news. Readers should log on to the portal's site, find readable news out of numerous unnecessary information. The recommendation for the news stays within the portal. If other friends want to see the recommendation results, those friends should come to the portal as well. Readers expressed their reactions in comments. However, they are also confined to the portal. The gatekeeping by collective intelligence is impossible on the portal. Independent users and individuals cannot produce news on the portal either.

## Every user is a master of social networks

On social networks, whether it is an individual or a media or a portal, all have the same status. On Twitter, both individuals and the media are allowed only 140 characters per posting. The media or portals can not intentionally set the fun or value of the posting. As users repeatedly shared the posting, the collective evaluation will occur in time. Frequently, a Twitter mention by an individual is more powerful than any other news reported by a media. On social networks, top headlines or sub-headlines on the internet site of a media do not mean anything. Recommended news on social networks operates in a completely separate system from the traditional newsroom. The newsroom cannot intervene in the news while the news spreads into peer groups.

Social networks can also generate news that has an enormous social impact. Important issue generate lots of sharing. Retweets on Twitter and Like buttons on Facebook go viral. The number of Retweets and Likes determines the significance of the issue. How much the issue is sensitive can be measured by the speed of the dissemination of the post. Although a media attempts to stress on an issue, it is not regarded as important as they intend. They need to earn recognition from individual users.

The opposite is true. Once an issue spreads on social networks, nobody can stop it. If one finds out a story is distorted and make corrections immediately, the issue will disappear quickly. There is no turning back. Here is why we need risk management on social networks. Because the speed is so fast, an issue spread once on the networks cannot be reversed. Thus, we can say that the control of the news has gone into the hands of users on social networks.

# 9. Story Building Journalism

## Newsroom? Story building room!

Journalists still have their competitiveness in story building. It will be beneficial for them to focus more on story building than article writing. To produce articles and to rebuild those through CPR for social-mobile media are two different things. A reporter, who can choose various platforms and build up a story, will lead to journalism in the era of social-mobile news. The reporter has to have one more skill -- distributing the news in the most appropriate channels at the right time. These skills are essential for a journalist in the era of social-mobile news.

It is the same case as a newsroom. A newsroom should be called "a story building room." The newsroom has focused only on the production of news. Once the news was produced, it was the end of the story. The distribution of the news was a linear, top-down process.

Reporters who belong to a newsroom go around their beats, discover issues and write articles. An editor reviews the articles. He screen and weighs them in editor meeting to decide where in the paper to put. Then layout editors make pages. The role of the newsroom ends here.

## USA Today appointed "executive editor for content distribution and programming"

In the era of social-mobile news, the news distribution channels are various and multi-dimensional. News is everywhere on social networks such as Facebook, small and large internet communities as well as news sites. Devices for news are also diversified. Consumers are moving fast from desktop PCs to smartphones. On top of this, there are tablet PCs and smart TVs.

New channels have different peak times according to user preference. They have various output forms and user behaviors. If you shove news to smart users in a standardized format in the old way, they will reject that news media. For smart readers, news articles bombarded on to them are just spams. They read the news at their convenience in the "ambient" environment.

To date, the traditional media have not been able to experience this sophisticated distribution of news. Custom-designed internet news site of course exists, but they have not been successful. The distribution of social news should be carefully designed in multi-dimensions. The newsroom has to play this role because it knows the news stories the best.

# The newsroom should not only produce news but manage news distribution

The trend has already emerged in reality. On August 26, 2010, US national daily USA Today announced its shift to a mobile-friendly organizational structure. The company said it was for "evolution from a newspaper company to a multi-platform media company." The company newly appointed executive editor for "content distribution and programming" to effectively distribute news on various information platforms including USA Today's paper, online and mobile media. The company also created a post, the vice president of digital development who focuses on developing and maintaining technology and systems. He supports the company's existing dot com, mobile, iPhone, and iPad platforms.

## Gathering news materials in a broad scope

The production of news now has become entirely different from that in the past. The linear structure where reporters gather facts and editors screen out is not competitive anymore in terms of content value. News now needs story building factors. The scope of the news sourcing should be set extensive, and story building should be done in the form of CPR.

We can categorize news materials into four. Firstly, there is open-sourced content produced by anyone on the internet. At second, there is social content created on social networks. Thirdly, there is original content provided by the media. The last is the affiliated content from other media.

These content in the four categories are all news content. What we should remember here is that they are just materials. There was only original content in the past for the news market, but now they are just part of news materials. Even though original content is a small part of news materials, they cost the highest among the four. It could sound very intimidating to reporters working for the traditional media. However, there is no other way to survive in the social-mobile news market but to widen the scope of news content. Now, we have to think about how to gather these four news materials effectively.

## A factory that assembles news components

A newsroom's task will be rather than producing articles but newly creating content from gathered information. It does not mean it should exaggerate or ignore facts. It should choose the most appropriate medium and rebuild the content and make the most multi-dimensional, exciting, and valuable story out of it. At the same time, the story can be re-processed in different formats depending on each smart device.

Sometimes they tried to shift the function of the newsroom from news production to story building. It was called "integrated newsroom." Its purpose was to create multimedia news by mixing various forms of media. The other important function of the integrated newsroom is news distribution. Internet webpages took a significant role in distributing news. It led newsrooms to change into an integrated newsroom.

You can call it an integrated newsroom or story building room. It should become a factory where you gather and process various materials to produce goods. Finished goods here are news stories formed in CPR. Among the four kinds of news materials, you can transform crowd-sourced content and social content into news stories through one of two steps of processing. The processing phase is a must for news production in the newsroom.

## Take one step higher as a "story builder"

There are two levels of processing news content. One is for a reporter who gathers facts and produces articles. At a higher level, a story builder who can process news materials while writing stories. It is up to individual skills. For a more completed story, a story builder's role is more significant. The role of editors of the existing newsroom should be taken by story builders now.

They can cut video clips or insert a QR code, for example, to process news for viral news consumption.

## The first step of story building: Restructuring

Story building occurs in two steps: the restructuring of news materials and the versioning for proper devices. In some cases, the two steps can occur simultaneously. A reporter carries out all the tasks from the start to the end. It is the most economical way. However, reporters would regard it as something difficult for the current news market, but it will become an ordinary task for smart reporters in the near future.

In the restructuring phase, we should decide a news format first -- whether it should be short straight news, detailed news, an interview, or a feature. After determining the format, we should choose which media we will use to make the news most effective. It can be a picture, traditional texts, texts with image or texts with a video. It all depends on the news. Please keep in mind that the consumers are smart readers.

## The second step of story building: Versioning

The next step is versioning. Whether it's a straight or a feature, news comes different on different smart devices, resulting in different user behaviors. We should take into account the user environment and behavior when restructuring stories in relevant formats.

We will treat those who can do all of the things above as professionals. Those who are used to CPR and story building will be the same level of the expert as journalists who could use CAR 15 years ago. It will not be easy to instantly know if the story should be a short straight or a feature. Moreover, you have to know simultaneously handle a variety of media tools and finish versioning in a short amount of time. However, if you do similar works repeatedly in the story building room, there will be "prototypes." Then, there will be various news templates in the story building room. News templates will have their respective codes. Under the leadership of an intermediary manager, the story building room will be able to mass-produce news content.

It will be played just like American football, as all team members instantly move at the quarterback's call of the play, under the lead of a coach. The quarterback's play call is three dimensional. For example, under the play call "I right 25," "I" refers to the offense formation, "right" refers to the side of the offense, and "25" means offense points of 2 and 5. Hearing play call, players check their positions and take actions in a matter of seconds. The story building room needs this kind of instant teamwork. If a creative play, coming once in a while, succeeds, it will bring a significant victory for the team.

## Three groups of human resources for newsroom

Up until now, we only talked about news production. There is still news distribution to be talked about. The other wing of the story building room is news distribution. Without proper distribution, versioning is pointless. With distribution in mind, an editor can effectively spread the news. I will go over the news distribution in a separate chapter later.

The story building room needs human resources different from those who worked at the newsroom.

First, it needs journalists with new skills, including the capacity to use the software in CPR, to research data on the internet and to comfortably use social networks.

Second, it needs editors or desk editors who can do storytelling in CPR. On top of the new skills mentioned above, editors should be able to restructure stories in a new way.

Third, it needs executive managers who catch changes in the news market, manage changes, and understand new business opportunities. In the fast-changing news market, they should be aware of how to sell news and have insights to grab new business opportunities in the news streams. This kind of human resources should manage the story building room.

When USA Today announced reorganization and restructuring, their No. 1 priority was vice president for business development. No. 2 was vice president for product development and design to improve the daily's "products." It also made a position for vice president for digital development and executive editor of content distribution in the newsroom.

## Smart readers are already aware of news components

What should smart readers do to make independent news content? They should hunt for issues, build stories, diffuse issues, collect feedbacks, and reproduce issues. The purpose is to send news content on the social stream and make the issue go viral.

Hunting for issues is not different from those done by traditional reporters. However, the content of issues has become quite different now. Traditional reporters usually go to their beats, meet people there, gather materials, and find issues there. However, smart readers find issues around them. The target or scope of issues is not limited. They think "something new happening to me is news to others."

Smart readers can also find new issues on people on their social networks. Social networks are another ecology where you tell your stories and consume others'. Without any medium, they share their stories directly. Various issues are updated every day. Those issues are selected and boosted by their friends. Smart readers find out what issues are meaningful, socially valuable, and personally interesting. Issues on social networks generate golden opportunities for news content. Moreover, hunting for issues on social networks costs zero. It can be very economical compared to the issue hunting in the era of offline papers.

The steps of story building include versioning -- fitting the news on smart devices. In the traditional newsroom, professional story builder used to do that for reporters. However, for smart readers, this task is not complicated. They are already used to using various platforms. So there is no need to distinguish storytelling, restructuring, and versioning separately.

# The life of the issue depends on reproduction

The next important step is the reproduction of the issue. It's about a decision when to distribute the news and when on which channel, after versioning. The timing is critical because different social networks have different user behaviors and peak times. According to the characteristics of the content, we can selectively choose which online community we will use to post. The traditional media did not pay attention to this phase. However, on social networks, it is just the beginning of the story. If we put news content on several channels, the lifecycle of the news finally begins.

After streaming the news, we should meticulously check on the feedbacks of readers. While monitoring feedbacks, we can find another opportunity to amplify the news content. We can discover new issues checking on Twitter mentions or quotes and comments on Facebook. It is often the case that feedbacks themselves break the news. In this case, the issue is regenerated over and over again, which will be the most successful case. It is an essential role of news producer on social-mobile to keep monitoring feedbacks and circulate issues. If the issue does not occur again, the life cycle of the news content ends.

# 10. Government directly talks through SNS

## Government briefings go mostly abandoned

It is journalists who get briefings from the government. Before a spokesperson gets ready for a briefing, he or she screens out issues that are not "newsworthy." The spokesperson only briefs what news media might write as news stories. Among many briefings from each department within the ministry, the spokesperson picks "newsworthy" ones.

Picking "newsworthy" materials mean throwing out "unimportant" materials. In most cases, most of them get abandoned. The spokesperson usually introduces only four or five issues at a regular briefing. Among those briefing to journalists, only a few of them get reported. On average, about three or four briefed issues become news stories per month, although some differences are depending on ministries.

Let's take an example of the Foreign Ministry of Korean government. The Ministry of Foreign Affairs and Trade has two regular briefings per week. At each briefing, the government announces four or five items. It means the ministry report 30-40 items in a month. Among them, only one or two things get reported in the media.

During October in 2011, the Foreign Ministry announced 30 issues through regular briefings. However, journalists picked up only two of them for their news stories. Q&As during the period got reported for seven news articles. Among the 30 briefings, 28 got abandoned.

Government briefings are meant to let Korean people know important issues, explain government policies and the government's stance on them. They only produce official content and do not have distribution power. The traditional media has distribution power instead.

Unreported briefed items die out without reaching people. Here, the government squanders a considerable amount of efforts. From the supply side, not being able to distribute briefings across the nation is a big waste.

From the demand side, not being able to learn significant issues or policies from the government is also a waste.

# It's not journalists who get briefed

The fundamental reason why there is so much waste in briefing items is that the traditional media has limited resources. Newspapers cannot put all kinds of stories on limited paper space. Broadcasters cannot report all types of news during a short news program, which usually lasts less than 1 hour. Most of TV news programs cover about 30 stories per day. All important issues should be narrowed down to 30, which is a minimal sampling. There is a serious bottleneck between supply and demand.

The social networks completely solved the bottleneck problem. It is the substance of the revolutionary change that social networks have brought in. Social networks can handle all kinds of numerous issues. They enable users to share and distribute stories directly. On social networks, anyone can announce a briefing item and distribute it. No matter how the small it can be, it will be shared among users as long as they regard it "important."

From the spokesperson's view, it will not be important to screen briefing items whether they are newsworthy on social networks because there is limitless space. The spokesperson's briefings can directly reach people bypassing journalists.

Can you imagine how much power social networks can have? The shift is beyond the change of production and distribution of issues. Readers' accepting behavior and culture have changed. Readers on social media want to hear directly from news sources, be it a press release, commentary, statement, or spokesperson's briefing. The demand is spiking up. It is a practical reason for the spokespersons of the government to shift targets from journalists to people.

# Conservatives poor at social communication

The conservatives in Korea have been deplorable at social communication. Their writing styles are excessively rough, aggressive, and crude. Most of their writings are rather emotional than sensitive to persuade the other side with logic and rationality. A majority of them are impossible to be published in newspapers.

Let me take a good example out of this. A by-election for Seoul Mayor was held on October 26, 2011. Conservatives' attacks began early in the morning. On social networking-based news media Wikitree, postings from the conservatives came one after another which mostly crudely attacked candidate Park Won-soon from the opposition party.

A social network user wrote a posting under the title "Park Won-soon sued for embezzlement of public funds." The posting said things like these; "Park received money from conglomerates and the rich by threatening and blackmailing them," "It would have been impossible for Park to check every receipt while spending billions of wons," "Park is the man who embezzles the money that originally had to go to the poor." Immediately after this posting was put up on Wikitree, the media company deleted the posting with a message to the writer saying, "We will delete this post because it contains slandering expressions." However, the writer uploaded the posting again. Wikitree inquired about this to an advisory lawyer. The lawyer said, "the posting has legal issues because it contains conclusive expressions as if unconfirmed stories of candidate Park Won-soon are facts." Finally, they deleted the posting.

Then, another post under the title, "Park Won-soon calls you a bad person if you don't give him money" was up on Wikitree. It contained vulgar expressions that are not appropriate to mention here. On the by-election day, the posting also had a message not to vote for Park. Wikitree also sent a similar message to the writer and deleted the post. Wikitree's lawyer said "the post also delivers a message to the moderate not to vote for Park, which is against the election law," adding that this kind of posting will not be able to be published on any newspaper.

On social networks, clumsy or inadequate political voices will not be heard but entirely blocked by users. The conservatives in Korea still don't get that.

## The homepage is not new media anymore

Be it a political party or the National Police Agency or the Foreign Ministry; it is difficult to make people hear their voice at the right time using the traditional media. If something negative comes up, they usually had to wait for another day to read newspapers the next morning or watch TV news and make response strategies. In the social-mobile era, they can voice themselves in real-time.

Online PR should be re-directed from websites to mobile social networks. Homepages are not new media anymore. The "one-to-many" structure with aggregated content waiting for readers to come is just another form of one-way media. Social media deals "many-to-many" relationships on the same status. Friends on social networks voluntarily spread exciting and useful stories.

In the social media era, the media should find readers by using social networks like Facebook and Twitter. The center of online PR should move to the Facebook fan page and use Twitter as a "propagation engine." Once we move the content of a homepage to social networks, the media find readers on a much broader scale. The number of readers of the social platforms, including Twitter, Facebook, Flikr, and YouTube, cannot be compared to that of the legacy media homepage.

When the internet became popular in 2000, people competitively tried to build their homepages. Now, almost anyone has a homepage. Social networks became popular in 2010. People again, competitively tried to build an effective system on social networks. For the next ten years, social networks will keep evolving, just like the internet did.

# 11. The era of social politics

## "Politicians should directly talk on the internet"

Chosun Monthly magazine in August 2008 ran a story titled, "Politicians, directly talk on the internet" when Koreans held a series of protests against U.S. beef imports. It was one year, and six months before Korea's first social networking news service Wikitree opened on February 2, 2919. It was even before the iPhone appeared in Korea. However, the 2008 U.S. beef protests signaled that "a huge change" began, shifting from "offline politics" to "online politics."

K-pop boyband TVXQ's fan page "Cassiopeia" gathered more than 800,000 teenagers to debate on U.S. beef imports, and some of them went out to Gwanghwamun in central Seoul to participate in demonstrations. They said they wanted to keep their school meals safe from possibly dangerous U.S. beef imports. However, then Lee Myung-bak administration countered protestants with "internet real-name system," requiring users to use their legal names. The Lee administration had to pay a high price because it did not realize the audience, and the method of politics have changed. Below is the article published by Chosun Monthly at that time.

"The rule of law was demolished not because the internet spread rumors or misinformation but because people's "rights to pursue happiness" have been fringed upon. President Lee said, "representative government" faces challenges due to people's aggressive participation in politics and the advancement of the internet." However, people's participation does not run against representative democracy. The reason why candle vigils became violent, public trust plunged, and the rule of law fell to the ground is because the Lee administration could not read "the huge change" in the audience and the method of politics. Thus, the government failed to do proper internet communication with people in the early stages of the protests."

## "Twitter users are defiant of authority"

The next day after the election for Seoul Mayor was over on Oct. 26, 2011, Hong Jun-pyo, then chairperson of the Grand National Party announced that the party would "hire a social networking service expert from outside and develop an application." However, the party did not see much fruitful result. SNS is not about a technique. It is a tool of communication. How can you improve communication by hiring an expert and develop an app?

It is not easy for the conservatives to be successful in operating SNS, just like prominent legacy newspapers like Chosun Ilbo find it challenging to do so. Many users of SNS do not want to communicate with conservative media. Of course, the opposition party is almost the same as the conservatives, in terms of political communication. Politicians declared statements such as "We would end the party politics," or "Old media died."

Then, chairperson Hong's attitude suddenly changed to attack social media users. He said people were living in an "insane society" where internet rumors spread wider than those written by the media. He said, "SNS users already have vested rights and cultural power." It was horrible that misinformation on SNS was regarded as facts and spread wide.

Then, almost all conservative groups started to attack SNS, including Twitter. They included the Presidential Office of Cheongwadae, Korea Communications Standards Commission, the Supreme Prosecutors' Office, the National Election Commission, and the conservative newspapers and broadcasters.

Chosun Ilbo said in a column titled, "What kind of citizens are we?" that 3,763 Twitter users uploaded 60 percent of tweets related to Seoul mayoral by-election. It also said their opinions were "turned into Seoul citizens' opinions." "SNS offers an easy and fast communication tool for many people, but it could easily go sensational by a small piece of wrong information. On Korea-U.S. FTA issues, there is much biased information floating around on SNS. On this kind of issue, a small number of demagogues can easily mislead citizens," the column said.

However, the column was far from the truth. The 3,763 Twitter users did not "uploaded" 60 percent of the tweets but "retweeted" others' postings which reached more than 4 million Twitter users in Korea.

It is what "communication" and "solidarity" mean on Twitter. It means participation-driven, solidarity-oriented democracy, and two-way communication by networked individuals. However, it is not that they exaggerated the opinions of the 3,763 users. Retweeted posts are either screened out or shared by "collective intelligence." It is just not possible to upload a posting and expect it to spread on social networks automatically.

If a "Twitter expert" can tweet about the election and it instantly reaches so many people, the Saenuri Party (formerly Grand National Party) will nurture 3,763 Twitter warriors. However, in reality, it will be tough to raise the number of retweets even if they could use 37,630 users because "collective intelligence" will refuse to do so. It's not about social networks. It's about communication. Politicians should do "good politics."

## Uncomfortable truths about SNS

Some say SNS turned politics into entertainment. Others fiercely debate whether it is "collective intelligence" or "collective conformity." However, the debate is pointless. The Korean "SNS generation" has already experienced their voluntary participation led to a victory in the election. They are "the new power."

Recent SNS users' political preference shows that many of them are against old powers, including Cheongwadae, the Saenuri Party, and the opposition party in Korea.

The traditional media is losing power. Their lost readers became media themselves using SNS and found solidarity through networks. Twitter users learned by themselves that they could make their voices heard without the traditional media.

Here is another uncomfortable truth about SNS. SNS is not a hotbed for leftists. Of course, there are many leftist voices on SNS in Korea. However, it is a natural phenomenon because the conservatives are in power, and major media are also conservative. In an interview with OhMyNews, American writer and social media evangelist Clay Shirky said people should not believe that many SNS users are progressive. He said these tools do not empower the progressives but those in the opposition side of the governing power. In other words, voluntary participants on SNS wield the power of checks and balances that the traditional media cannot do.

Shirky took an opposite example of U.S. politics. He said while the Obama administration could not make use of social media in wielding policies as much as it did during the presidential election, far-right Tea Party was using social media to put pressure on the government. News reports about Tea Party's political movement had been very limited on major U.S. newspapers in the past, but it had no problem in PR after it used social media to hold free conference calls and secure e-mail lists, Shirky said.

In other words, SNS was a useful tool for Americans to choose Barack Obama of the Democratic Party over John McCain of the Republican Party, in punishment of the Bush administration. Also, SNS was an excellent tool for Americans who were disappointed by the Obama government to support the right-wing Tea Party.

SNS is where collective intelligence works. It is straightforward to open an account on Twitter or Facebook, but the membership does not guarantee anonymity. Networked users try to save their face and hope their postings make an impact on social networks. Sometimes postings can be too graphic, but most of the time, they desire the greater good.

Highest-ranking tweets are those retweeted by collective intelligence. The criteria are whether it has "common sense or not," not "conservative vs. liberal."

## Chosun Ilbo makes the wrong accusation

The conservatives in Korea stigmatized SNS as "an epicenter of rumors." However, the more they stigmatize it, the stronger the resistance they get. On Nov. 16, 2011, Chosun Ilbo published an article titled, "Kang Ho-dong died? SNS went too far" after a tweet saying "Kang Ho-dong found breathing at his house this morning (urgent)" went viral and the popular entertainer's name was trending on major portals.

The newspaper said false suicide rumors on celebrities are circulating social networks, adding that Kang Ho-dong's suicide rumor quickly spread on Twitter. However, the initial tweet was just a wordplay, switching the word "숨진" (dead) to "숨쉰" (breathing). Most of Twitter users regarded it as a brilliant wordplay and even made other wordplay parodies. Users in the end mocked Chosun Ilbo's article.

## Groundless rumors spread on SNS? It's a myth

The most noticeable difference between the traditional media and SNS is the process of correcting stories. The important thing is how the wrong article gets corrected and how unbiased the correction is. Surprisingly, stories are corrected faster and more precisely on SNS than on the traditional media. The traditional media are very hesitant at fixing their stories.

In this sense, SNS with collective intelligence offers a better communication sphere than the traditional media. There is no authoritarian individual to wield editorial power on SNS because participants evenly dispersed. It is the "democratized editorial right." Among more than 4 million users, experts correct any wrong tweets with their expertise. This mechanism automatically reduces misinformation or distorted stories, just like Wikipedia works.

An individual is media on social networks. As individual media, people bring change to society and reform the world. They have the desire to participate in the process of making the world better. Therefore, users have a "refining power" to delete, block, or correct posts quickly. It is just groundless that SNS spreads groundless rumors.

## Opinion poll without tweet analysis goes off the mark

Now, it has become almost impossible to predict election results by conducting an opinion poll on the phone. Most households do not use landlines anymore. Even if they do, 70 percent of their numbers are not registered. Maybe we can trust only exit polls at voting sites.

However, going in the opposite direction of this trend, Rep. Koh Seung-duk of then ruling Grand National Party in 2011 submitted a revision bill of the election law, which bans the announcing or reporting of opinion polls on voters six days before the election. He said six days should be reduced to three days because SNS should come under control.

In reality, media polls on predictions of the Seoul Mayor election showed Rep. Na Kyung-won of then Grand National Party nearly caught an independent Park Won-soon or even surpassed Park in the support rate. On SNS, however, Na never surpassed in terms of the number of tweets. Broadcaster MBC's deputy managing editor said the media's polls are not credible, adding that Park has been leading the poll by about 10 percent point gap from Na. Later in the election, Park beat Na with a 7.2 percent point gap in votes.

As the frequency of tweets about candidates positively related to the actual votes, polling experts and statistics professionals make use of social media as an alternative tool for polling. Some companies analyze social data and "buzz" on SNS to predict a result of elections and provide them for each politician's campaign.

## Twitter users post selfies after voting

Social networks, including Twitter, directly affect elections. It has already been proved that Twitter is the most influential media in reporting natural disasters and elections. When natural disasters such as flood and earthquake occur, people tend to get access on Twitter than visiting media websites. On election days, people talk about candidates with numerous others on social media. On the election day, social media becomes a reliable medium to encourage voters to go voting.

At the local elections in Korea on June 2, 2010, Twitter proved that it could encourage people to vote. It was the day when Korean people started posting selfies immediately after voting. One Twitter user on May 31, two days before the election day, suggested users join in posting evidence selfie on Twitter after voting, with a hashtag "#62vote." Wikitree retweeted this, adding a mention that it will give out 20 boxes of dried seaweed to those who upload their selfies after voting. The event went viral and affected other celebrities to encourage voting by promising other eventful gifts. Visual artist Lim Ok-sang offered his prints to 1,000 people in their 20s, poet Ahn Do-hyeon, 30 copies of his book "The Salmon Who Dared to Leap Higher" and actor Kwon Hae-hyo, 20 tickets of play "Love Letter."

# Selfies at voting sites get trending on SNS

On the local election day on June 2, selfies began to come up early in the morning. As soon as voting sites opened at 7 a.m., users posted their selfies after voting. Korean law prohibits to shoot a picture of the inside of a voting box or a ballot. Users adviced each other to keep them from infringing the election law.

Then, an exciting photo was up. A young couple took the selfie together after voting, uploaded it, and said the wife was expecting a baby on that day. The husband again uploaded a photo of a newborn a couple of hours later, saying their third child was born. The photo on Twitter received explosive mentions congratulating the birth as well as encouraging others who have not voted yet to go voting. A tweet saying, "if you don't vote after seeing this picture, you're not even a person" got retweeted all over Twitter.

Celebrities joined the selfie movement. The first celebrity who posted an "evidence photo" of voting was actress Park Jin-hee. Then, comedian Jeong Jong-cheol, singer Kim Chang-ryeol, Girls' Generation member Yuna and MC Kim Je-dong followed suit. Powerful Twitter user and novelist Lee Oi-soo also posted his selfie after voting.

# 630,000 Twitter users move up voting rates

As the elections went on, voting rates started to move up. After remaining low in the morning, they began to pick up in the afternoon. The national voting rate in 2010 local elections as of 6 p.m. increased to 54.5 percent from 51.6 percent in 2006 elections.

Around the time of June 2, 2010, local elections, there were about 630,000 Twitter users in Korea, mostly in the Seoul Metropolitan area. The "selfie proof" movement led young voters to the voting sites. They were indifferent to politics. However, Twitter turned to vote into a "play" and made young voters voluntarily enjoy the election. The voting rate analysis officially proved it. The National Election Commission announced the result of the analysis on Aug. 26, 2010, and said the voting rates among those in their 30s and younger groups increased, while those among voters over 40 decreased.

In particular, 19-years-old voters' voting rate spiked by 9.5 percent points compared to the 2006 local elections.

## "Voting after work" becomes a fad

By-elections on April 27, 2011, also showed a new phenomenon. Because the election day was Wednesday and not designated as a national holiday, working people went voting after work. Twitter users encouraged workers to vote. The voting rate went up by 1 or 2 percentage points per hour on average during the election day. However, between 7-8 p.m., it jumped by 6.3 percentage points. In Bundang area near Seoul, the 10,398 votes between 7-8 p.m. accounted for 12.7 percent of the total votes.

## Last-minute voting rush by youth on the subway

We witnessed another interesting phenomenon on the primary election on Oct 3, 2011, when the opposition camp was to decide a unified candidate for Seoul mayoral by-election between Rep. Park Young-sun of the Democratic Party and an independent Park Won-soon. It was a last-minute voting rush by young people, who mostly took a subway to get to the voting site in Jangchung Gymnasium in Seoul.

In the morning that day, large tourism buses carried groups of senior voters to the voting site. As senior voters tended to vote for Park of the Democratic Party, young Twitter users encouraged their peers to vote for Park Won-soon in the afternoon.

One tweet said, "The voting rate did not exceed 30 percent as of 1 p.m., which leaves candidate Park Won-soon in a risky situation. Let's go to Jangchung Gymnasium to vote."

Oct 3 was the National Foundation Day. On holidays, young Koreans usually do not bother to vote and go out and play instead. However, tweets encouraging voting on Oct 3, 2011, actually pushed up the voting rate to 39.7 percent as of 3 p.m., and to 59.6 at the final hour of 9 p.m., Park Won-soon won the ticket to Seoul mayoral race.

# Last-minute voting rush helps Park win Seoul mayoral election

The last-minute voting rush occurred again on the Seoul mayoral election day on Oct 26, 2011. The turnout was a decisive factor of the race between Park Won-soon and Na Kyung-won of then Grand National Party.

The voter participation in three wealthy districts in Seoul -- Seocho, Gangnam and Songpa -- was higher than expected. Many GNP supporters in the three districts went voting in the morning. Then, at around 15:50, the Park Won-soon's camp suddenly announced that it would hold an urgent press briefing. At 16:00, the camp's spokesperson said the camp is urging voters across the nation to cast ballots. It is against the law to do campaigning on the election day because it can affect election results. However, the urgent press briefing was a strategic move to encourage voting bypassing the election law. The briefing was reported all over the media, and the news quickly spread on social networks. Then, the last-minute voting rush after work occurred again. From 7 p.m. to 8 p.m., just an hour before the closing, the voter participation went up by 5.7 percentage points.

# Korean election law regards Twitter as "kind of e-mail"

Twitter has become influential in elections. Candidates strategically make use of Twitter as a useful campaigning tool. It is unimaginable to see an election without Twitter now. Ordinary citizens, not just candidates or campaigning staffs, send political messages on Twitter or Facebook by supporting or opposing a candidate. However, the election law has not evolved into an up-to-date state yet.

Korea's election law is still controversial due to its vagueness on SNS issues. Under the current law, Twitter is regulated as "electronic mail" when preliminary candidates conduct campaigns. If they found unlawful information, recipients can request the information provider to stop, delete, or limit the information.

Unlike e-mail, however, Twitter does not fully disclose the personal information of users. It is also difficult to trace the original tweet sender when the tweets go viral with retweets. If there is an issue, users have to reach Twitter, the service provider located in the U.S., for cooperation. Moreover, it is hard to pinpoint, which is a simple expression of opinions and which is an election campaign within the limit of 140 letters.

## National Election Commission admits vagueness in tweet crackdown

The National Election Commission admitted that it had vague criteria when regulating election campaign-related tweets. To evaluate if a particular posting on Twitter is considered an election campaign, the NEC said it has to thoroughly analyze a tweet's content, motive, purpose, timing, and frequency.

The NEC said they would consider the expressing users' preference to a specific candidate by referencing the candidate's personality or experience as a "simple opinion," while urging other users to "spread this message" or to "promote this message" as campaigning.

 Because it is difficult to come up with a standardized measure to control election-related tweets, the NEC tends to release election law violation cases frequently. The NEC said it acknowledges Twitter users' ability to weed out malicious comments on individual candidates, as users tend to share their followers of identities altogether. However, due to the vague criteria, users are still worried that the NEC may hurt freedom of expression on social media during election time.

## "Cyber Election Malpractice Watchdog" caught by Twitter users

Before the Seoul mayoral election in 2011, a Twitter account under the name, "Cyber Election Malpractice Watchdog," appeared on Twitter and started following about 150 leftist Twitter accounts. Users raised suspicion that the watchdog account began monitoring left-wing Twitter users only.

On Oct 12, one Twitter user openly said to the watchdog account, "Can you clarify if this account is official from Seoul City's National Election Commission and what is the purpose of following me?" The watchdog account replied, "I am a member of the Cyber Election Malpractice Watchdog under the NEC, but I randomly picked whom to follow through googling by keyword Seoul Mayoral By-election." It added that it did not mean to do anything on Twitter but offer election-related information.

One person makes a direct phone call to the NEC to complain about being followed on Twitter. Other Twitter users asked the cyber watchdog account to unfollow them.

As people kept complaining about the watchdog account, the NEC finally deleted it at around 5 p.m. on that day. Twitter users thwarted NEC's move to monitor Twitter users.

# Celebrity posts dog photo to bypass election law violation

Taking photos after voting comes under the scrutiny of the authorities, whether it violates the election law. Taking a photo inside of the voting box is illegal. Taking a photo of the ballot or posting it on social media is also a violation of the election law. However, it is okay to take a photo of an empty ballot.

Posting a selfie shot in front of the voting site which does not recommend voting for a specific candidate has nothing to do with the election law. However, if the photo indicates in any way that it promotes a particular candidate, it can violate the law.

The NEC's statement on banning celebrities from posting selfies on the election day faced fierce criticism. The NEC said, "we will ban some celebrities from recommending people to vote on the election day because, for some of the celebrities, recommending itself may indicate inducing people to vote for a certain candidate."

According to the NEC, it was against the law for a celebrity to post a selfie on Twitter to encourage voting, but it was not against the law to say he or she had already voted to post a selfie. However, the NEC did not offer a clear answer on who could define "some celebrities" come under the category and what was the difference between encouraging people to vote before voting and after voting.

Celebrities then bypassed the election law. MC Kim Je-dong took his selfie only half of his face, and singer Lee Hyo-ri took the photo of her dog in front of the voting site. When offering event prizes for voting, the post should not designate a particular party, region, or age group. One person got sued for providing a reward to voters in their 20s in local elections on June 2, 2010. However, offering rewards for all voters do not violate the law.

## Legal issues on Twitter should be solved on Twitter

The NEC understands well about social networks. Even if social network users do not reveal their real names, people try to save face in many-to-many communication space. On social networks, "reputation risk" exists.

First of all, users themselves refrain from using graphic expressions. It is just like in reality; they cannot spit out bad words in front of many people. If there is excessive use of foul words, many other users instantly take issues with it.

The NEC understands this very well. Initially, it asks the tweet uploader to delete the message. If the user refuses to do so, the NEC request help from the police, then, the commission collects similar cases and expose them on the internet.

Twitter users are aware that they have a "reputation risk." It would be better for the NEC to make use of the social network system itself. For example, it can not only send a mention to the violator but openly spread an official reply to share with other users the cause of the violation and correction requests. It can be most effective among Twitter users.

 By doing so, the NEC will also be able to learn what other Twitter users think about the NEC's decision and lead them in the right direction concerning the election law. Collecting many examples at one place on a website does not work effectively.

We could see the automatic "refining system" on Twitter in many Twitter interviews. While Twitter users watch the whole process of the interview on

Twitter, they can openly request to stop using harsh or violent words in real-time. It can play a strong deterrent to language abuse for other users. The NEC can learn a great deal out of this.

# 12. Social Advertisement

## Social advertisement, collectively created and distributed

The key to social networks is people's participation and sharing. "Social advertisement" refers to advertisement created and distributed by the engagement of the people. It is entirely different from existing ads. In the past, there was no role of readers to play in the process of producing or publishing ads. However, on social networks, readers directly evaluate ads. They collaborate to find out whether ads are exaggerated or false. If they find it useful, they share the advertisement with positive comments. If an ad gets adverse reactions, it will be a severe risk to the company.

The traditional media had to make a clear distinction between news and ads so that readers do not confuse the two. Newspapers run an ad and distribute papers to readers. If readers think the ad is not based on facts, they can make a phone call and complain about it. However, they could not make other readers to learn it because they did not connect with each other. In this structure, newspapers had to set up a separate ethics guidance for a newspaper advertisement.

In the era of social networks, readers connected in real-time. About any content produced by a media, anyone can make a judgment and comment about it. They do not need to distinguish whether it is news or ad. They need to know if it is true or false, useful, or harmful. Many other readers evaluate as a group. The linear system where the media was involved in content production, distribution, and feedback management do not exist anymore.

Of course, people could send feedbacks to comments or bulletin boards of media websites in the past. However, comments are not two-way interactions but one-way communication between a single media and many readers. To learn about other feedbacks, readers should find the website and search for the article's comments. Moreover, the media controls the comments which put the media on the upper status.

The control over content evaluation and judgment now is in the hands of the people. The media decides whether the content is valuable or not. Then, readers will evaluate on the screened content. This kind of system has a virtuous function that an excellent product or service can be quickly spread among smart readers. A bad product is instantly blocked. For consumers, reputation on social networks is the most important criteria when choosing a product.

## Sell social stream

So-called "advertorial," a blend of advertisement and editorial, has had a negative connotation. On social networks, however, there is no need to distinguish them as advertorials. It will be up to readers to judge whether it is news or advertisement or advertorial. With the change in the concept, some websites are already doing related business for profits. Danish trendsetting site Baekdal.com publish sponsored articles. A sponsored article, priced at $250 per article, introduces the sponsor in the first part of it and has the link to the sponsor.

As users' evaluations have become an essential part of PR on social networks, advertisers should have a new strategy in managing PR content. In short, it should be "content first." It is risky to promote a product or service from the first place explicitly. The advertiser should make customers understand the product's fundamental values, and then, offer detailed information about the product. If customers' reactions are not enthusiastic in the first phase, the advertiser should start from scratch and persuade them again. Without the understanding of fundamental values, pushing the product or service to the customers is like a suicide. Therefore, an advertorial is a must.

To make this strategy successful, the advertiser should make a stream of content on social networks. Once the content is published, it should be spread through the hands of readers and generate feedbacks. While monitoring the social stream, the advertiser can measure how fast and wide the content has spread. They can also check how consumers react by looking at their comments, often added when sharing the content. The comments are valuable feedbacks offered in real-time. The prerequisite for this process is that the content should flow on "social stream." Media should sell this "social stream" to advertisers.

# Limitless combinations of social advertisement and mobile

Social advertisements are extensively various. After social networks met mobility, the variety reached a peak. The imagination of advertisement producers is the only untapped area in the era of social-mobile. From now on, it is possible to run a low-cost and high-efficiency advertisement. When social networks based on collaboration and sharing meet multifunctional mobile devices, they will create infinite possibilities for the social ad. Anyone can create an ad.

On social networks, we should make all content mobile-friendly. It also applies to the advertisement. The social-mobile advertisement will be the most significant form of advertisement in the ad market. It is just like smartphones became the most important device for news consumption. We have to remind that mobile devices, such as smartphones and tablet PCs, have entirely different functions and characteristics from desktop PCs. Advertisers should pay attention to the following features of mobile devices.

- **Mobility**: It is the most fundamental characteristic. Mobile devices do not stay at a place. Wherever users go, they follow.

- **Portability**: Users always carry their mobile devices -- in a pocket, a purse and anywhere users can reach any time.

- **Location**: Mobile devices recognize their exact location with the help of GPS signals. Advertisement providers, however, should get agreement from mobile device users to use their location information. Using the location information, a local advertisement for consumers in a specific region is possible.

- **Timing**: Mobile devices offer the exact timing information which is necessary for timing-oriented ads and campaigns. It can be used for count-down campaigns as well. The duration factor, based on time and date, can be used for ads.

- **Sensing**: Mobile devices such as iPhone 6 has a gyroscope sensor that senses angles and velocity of the movement in three dimensions. Smartphones sense brightness, the intensity of noise, strength on the touch screen, and weight. Applying accurate senses to the advertisement will make it possible to run ads that excite five senses.

- **Augmented Reality**: It's a new world that smartphones brought together. It refers to a technology to show a camera view with layouts of computer-generated sensory input such as video or GPS data. It can show, for example, directions to a certain point, set by advertisers using location information. Putting a smartphone over a movie still cut on paper can show moving video on the screen. AR is the most influential factor to stimulate advertisement producers' imagination.

- **Multimedia**: On mobile devices, all kinds of media such as texts, pictures, video, sound, audio, and music are playing their roles. It gives us a significant meaning that anyone can easily produce good content using multimedia. A smartphone enables makings of high-definition videos and high-quality audio files in long-duration with ease. Consumers can openly participate in ad campaigns in the multimedia environment.

- **Engagement**: Engagement is the biggest asset of social networks. Consumers actively intervene in the distribution of ads. They also engage in the production of ads, thanks to the high performance of mobile devices. From the perspective of advertisers, they can directly run ad campaigns bypassing a newspaper or a broadcasting company. They can directly distribute social advertisements to social network users.

- **Programming**: We can attach a particular computer program to every ad. If we put together various features of mobile devices using an application, we can make ads that play like an interactive game. We can create a compelling ad through the programming of sensing, AR, GPS data, calling, and message sending functions.

- **Communication**: The primary function of a smartphone is phone calls. With wireless internet, audio or data communication is almost always available. When we make social-mobile advertisement, we have to always keep in mind that users can make a phone call or surf the internet at any time. We do not have to make users write down the phone numbers appeared on smartphone ads. We can put a button, linked with a phone call, on the ad, just like we do not put URL on banner ads on the internet.

- **Interactivity**: Consumers almost always connected on social networks through mobile devices, not only each other but with advertisers one to one. They can react to advertisers' mentions and raise complaints at any time. At the same time, they can have conversations with advertisers and other consumers.

- **Real-time**: Keep in mind that lots of consumers connected on social networks real-time. It is significant because feedbacks occur fast. The real-time significantly affects the dissemination of ads. If negative feedbacks spread on an advertisement or a campaign, risk management becomes crucial. It is not easy to deal with real-time chain reactions. Sports beverage brand Gatorade's Mission Control

Center monitors social networks 24 hours a day. Advertisements on social networks have become "instant ones."

## Advertisement department should become "creative marketing room"

An enormous change in the ad market will push the media industry to change the way they run ad business. The ad sales based on the media's authority and influence will not be useful anymore. The collapse of the oligopolistic media industry brought a significant change in the ad market.

When several media companies dominated the news market, advertisers themselves asked newspapers to publish their ads. Advertisement departments were taking phone calls from them. Then, the competition among media companies got fierce, and media companies used their media power to attract ads. Advertisers, who could not even check how the ads were effective, had to bit the bullet and give ads to the media. The traditional media's advertisement department stayed that way for a while.

However, in the advent of social networks, advertisers found a breakthrough. They could directly meet consumers, have conversations with them, and show them ads. As seen in the successful example of social ad "Old Spice" on YouTube, Twitter, and Facebook bypassing media companies, an international campaign that will shake the global market is now possible.

We should transform the existing advertisement departments of media companies into an organization helping corporate marketing. The organization should offer a content strategy to help corporate PR and marketing and secure networks to execute the strategy. In the organization, there should be marketers, not ad sales employees. It should come up with creative ideas to support corporate customer-oriented services. It should transform itself into a "creative marketing room."

Now, advertisers do not want simple ads on newspapers or banners on websites. Ads should be the medium to interact with consumers directly and receive consumer feedback in real-time. Advertisers are already interested in the social stream, and some of them have already made ads on the social stream.

Advertisement departments of the traditional media should be reorganized to function as marketing strategy developer. It should create marketing strategies that fit the social-mobile environment and present them to companies. If it fails to do so, advertisers will bypass the media and execute PR and marketing on social networks themselves.

If the traditional media still want to earn ad revenue, they should play a particular role in the social-mobile environment. The most significant part of the role is to develop creative PR and marketing strategies and present them to companies. To execute the strategy, they should also be able to reach collaboration with outside institutions and experts. Social advertisement is not something a single media company can do by itself. We should change the function of an advertisement department to a collaboration system for corporate marketing on social-mobile environment.

## Ads that "run or kill"

However, the most significant challenge for existing advertisement departments of media companies comes from somewhere else -- it is individuals. Individuals on social media will make inroads into the ad market. Smart readers will sweep the social ad market. Individuals who only received ads will be participants in creating ads. They will produce ads, approach to advertisers, and publish advertisements.

The environment to produce social ads is already open to smart readers. Without expensive equipment or software, anyone can create a high-quality video with a smartphone. Smart readers use their ideas to create ads that fit a particular company. There is no cost but imagination and time. Then, they offer them to the company. If the company is satisfied with the outcome, it pays the creator and publishes it on social networks. The publisher can be the company or the smart reader or employees of the company. If the company doesn't like it, the smart reader can kill it.

There are many social ads created in this way. Companies can receive numerous ad videos made by users. All they have to do is to decide whether to run the ad or not. Even if they do, it will not cost as much as TV commercials. From the side of the smart reader, it will not be a significant loss, either. Except for the time, the cost is almost zero. From the side of the company, it can purchase scores or hundreds of social ads. They can not only buy social ads but distribute them on social networks. In the case of "Old Spice," the commercial led to the production of 183 follow-up ads because the production cost was not much, and the distribution fee on social networks was zero.

On the social-mobile environment, it will be merely a game of "run or kill." If users of social-mobile take an ad, it will be put up on social networks and if not, killed. This kind of social ads will fundamentally change the ad market.

## "I am a media"

With the same status with the traditional media in the news market, smart readers directly participate in the ad market. It is possible because everyone is media. It is a revolutionary change that social-mobile era has brought. The traditional news and ad markets have collapsed. In the social-mobile era, anyone can write and distribute at the same time.

Moreover, they can manage feedbacks. Anyone can make ads, sell them, or discard them. A simple smartphone, imagination, and social networks are all it takes. In the social-mobile era, you have to remember, "I am a media."

# Huney Kong

## currently
CEO / Publisher, Social News Co., Ltd / Wikitree, the most influential internet news service in Korea
Adjunct Professor, Department of Media Arts & Sciences, Korea National Open University

## former
CEO, Nexus Investment Co., Ltd, *KOSDAQ listed venture capital*
Chief Information Officer, MoneyToday, *the first online financial news service in Korea*
Washington Correspondent, The Chunchu News Syndicate *by the five major local newspapers in Korea*
Reporter, Editor-in-chief, The Kwangju Ilbo Daily News

## academics
Master of Information Management and Systems, School of Information, UC Berkeley
Trained in Faculty of Journalism, Moscow National University
Master of Politics, Department of International Relations, Seoul National University
Bachelor of International Politics, Department of International Relations, Seoul National University

## books
*Media Innovation and News Storytelling (2019)*
*SNS Likes Stories (2017)*
*Do Politics by Social Networks (2015)*
*Watch, Listen, and Do News (2010)*
*Digital News Handbook (2000)*

All books above published in Korean